ALL-TERRAIN
PUSHCHAIR WALKS
Yorkshire Dales

Rebecca Terry

Published by Sigma Leisure – an imprint of
Sigma Press, 5 Alton Road, Wilmslow, Cheshire SK9 5DY, England.

British Library Cataloguing in Publication Data
A CIP record for this book is available from the British Library.

ISBN: 978-1-85058-831-3 (13 digit); 1-85058-831-7 (10 digit)

Typesetting and Design by: Sigma Press, Wilmslow, Cheshire.

Cover Photograph: Old Moor Lane, Grassington Moor Lead Mine Trail *(Copyright, Phillip Elsdon).*

Maps and graphics: Rebecca Terry

Photographs: Rebecca Terry, Phillip Elsdon & Tracy Whale

Printed by: Bell and Bain Ltd, Glasgow

Disclaimer: the information in this book is given in good faith and is believed to be correct at the time of publication. No responsibility is accepted by either the author or publisher for errors or omissions, or for any loss or injury howsoever caused. Only you can judge your own fitness, competence and experience. Do not rely solely on sketch maps for navigation; we strongly recommend the use of appropriate Ordnance Survey (or equivalent) maps.

Preface

The spectacular and varied scenery of the Yorkshire Dales covers a large area of North Yorkshire. In this book I have included walks from both the Yorkshire Dales National Park and Nidderdale, an area of outstanding natural beauty. There are an abundance of beautiful riverside walks, high level moorland rambles and strolls around the many country estates, castles and abbeys. With so much to see and do this makes the perfect location in which to introduce your children to walking. It is great to get them out and about as early as possible so that they can experience the delights of the world around them. An early introduction to walking also gives them an understanding of their surrounding environment and a healthy outlook for the future.

The advent of all terrain pushchairs means that there is now no reason why having a baby should deter us from enjoying the outdoors. However, the Yorkshire Dales are renowned for their dry stone walls and, therefore, the abundance of ladder and gap styles can make walking with a pushchair problematic. It is very difficult to plan a walk from a map as details of terrain and stiles are not available. But I have selected thirty tried and tested pushchair-friendly walks in the Yorkshire Dales, so that it is now possible to go for a walk with full knowledge of the route ahead.

In choosing these thirty walks I have tried to select a diverse range of scenery to show you the best that the Yorkshire Dales has to offer. I have also included a range of walk grades, from simple low-level strolls to more ambitious moorland stomps, so there is something for everyone. The 'at a glance' key makes walk selection easy and also gives information on refreshments etc, allowing you to plan ahead. Every walk has background information about the area and a selection of other ways to amuse the kids while you are there.

I have had great fun putting these walks together and hope that you and your children enjoy them as much as Jamie and I did.

Acknowledgements

Thanks to Jamie for making these walks so much fun and to Phil for all his help especially with the photos. Thanks also to all the other people who helped along the way especially Becks and Molly.

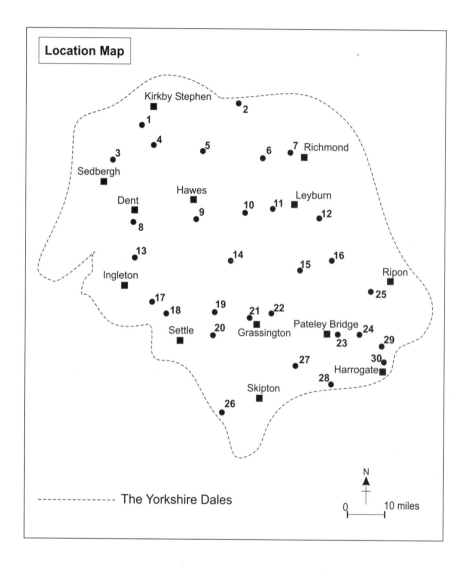

Location Map

Kirkby Stephen

- 2

- 1

- 4

Sedbergh
- 3

- 5

- 6
- 7 Richmond

Hawes

Dent
- 9

Leyburn
- 10
- 11

- 8
- 12

- 13

- 14

- 16

- 15
Ripon

Ingleton
- 25

- 17

- 18

- 19

- 21
- 22

Pateley Bridge
- 24

Settle
- 20
Grassington
- 23
- 29

- 27
- 30

- 28
Harrogate

Skipton

- 26

N

-------- The Yorkshire Dales

0   10 miles

Contents

Introduction

This book contains thirty walks in the Yorkshire Dales suitable for an all-terrain pushchair. The Yorkshire Dales are renowned for their wild and open moorland and dry stone walls. You may think that these features would make it unsuitable for pushchair walks but once you know where to go the opportunities are endless.

There are both circular and "there-and-back" routes, and many can be shortened or have worthwhile detours. Walks range from 1 to 5 miles in length and cover a wide range of difficulty thus catering for all types of walkers. The walks encompass the whole of the Yorkshire Dales National Park and Nidderdale, so, hopefully, you will find a suitable walk nearby, wherever you are. The walks are not exhaustive and are intended as an introduction to the area. There are many other suitable routes to explore once you know what is possible with a pushchair.

Routes and Grades

I have purposefully made this book as easy to follow as possible. Each walk is accompanied by a simple route map showing the start point and numbers referring to details in the text, as well as obvious features. The maps are intended to be used in conjunction with the relevant Ordnance Survey Explorer map, and the information on them is by no means comprehensive. Details of the relevant map and the starting grid reference are given in the walk summary.

Each walk contains an "at-a-glance" key which tells you all you need to know to prepare for the walk – distance, difficulty, any stiles, facilities such as toilets or ice cream vans and any hidden costs, so there shouldn't be any nasty surprises when you set off. You can also see whether the walk requires two people to overcome obstacles or if it can be accomplished solo.

The walks have a basic summary, detailing points of interest and useful information on the area. I have also included an "in the area" section, suggesting nearby alternative activities for yourself and your family.

You should always allow more time than that recommended. Times given are approximate and based on a speed of two miles an hour. However, not everyone walks at the same speed and the times given do not make allowances for picnics, tantrum breaks or walking toddlers.

It should be noted that circular routes are written in the direction which requires the least effort and are not always reversible! If you are thinking of reversing a walk, read the description carefully to check it is possible.

Fitness

It is assumed that walkers will have a basic level of fitness. Those who consider themselves unfit should only attempt the easiest level of walk and, if necessary, take advice from their doctor. The hardest level of walk should only be attempted by those experienced in both mountain walking and all-terrain pushchair technique.

All-Terrain Pushchairs
– Advice for First-Time Buyers

There are now many makes of all-terrain pushchairs (ATPs) on the market. For help in choosing an ATP, here are some of the factors I have come across in researching this and other books!

Ensure your child is old enough for the ATP. Many makes have a reclining position suitable for use from birth, but bear in mind that very young babies should not be bumped around. Seek the manufacturer's advice and choose your walks carefully. Small babies (less than four months) should only be taken on the easiest level of walks and if you are not happy with the terrain, turn round!

Make sure the ATP has pneumatic tyres and good suspension to provide cushioning.

Lightweight prams are better! There are a wide variety of ATPs on offer so try a few before you buy as some of the heavy ones are difficult to manoeuvre.

Choose a long wheel-base, which makes leverage over obstacles easier than a short wheel-base. The front wheel should be fixed, or, at the very least, lockable. Rear wheels should be quick release.

Check the pushchair folds easily and that it fits in the boot of your car!

Shop around as it is always worth looking in the shops first and then checking the internet for the same pram at a better price – either new or used.

Accessories

A **rain cover** is essential, especially when out walking in the hills, as the weather can change very quickly. Good quality **footmuffs** are easily available, if not already included in the price; fleece-lining and/or wind-proofing provides extra comfort.

Sunshades supplement the hood, which generally doesn't extend enough for walking uphill into full sun. Mesh shades are easier to walk with than parasols.

A **puncture repair kit** and **pump** are strongly advisable for those emergency situations. You can also fill the tyres with a "goo" designed as an emergency fix for bicycle tyres which prevents serious deflation.

A **pram leash** is useful, especially on walks with steep drops or steep descents. This is a strap, climbing sling or piece of rope tied to the pram handle and fastened to the wrist. This provides extra security should you accidentally let go of the pushchair, and is more secure than a handbrake.

Single and Double All-Terrain Pushchairs from the 'Mountain Buggy' range. *Reproduced by permission of Chariots All-Terrain Pushchairs www.pushchairs.co.uk*

What to take

For the baby:

✳ Pram with rain cover, sun cover, footmuff and puncture repair kit.

✳ Milk – if you are not breastfeeding, formula milk is easily carried in ready-made cartons or powder sachets; just add to water in bottles when you need it. If your baby likes warm milk, either carry warm water in a flask or make up extra hot milk and wrap in foil or a muslin.

✳ Nappies, wipes and nappy bag.

✳ Picnic – sandwiches are easy if your baby eats on his/her own, otherwise take fruit pots, yoghurt or anything easy to open. Don't forget a spoon and take all rubbish home with you.

✳ Snacks to cheer up a bored or peckish baby until you find a picnic spot. Raisins or baby crisps seem to keep them occupied for the longest!

✳ Water/juice

✳ Spare clothes. Layers are best as they can easily be put on or taken off as conditions change. Don't forget that though you may be hot walking uphill, your baby is sat still in the pushchair. Keep checking he/she is not too cold. An all-in-one fleece is a good buy. Look for one with fold-over ends to keep hands and feet warm – easier than gloves.

✳ Hat, either a sunhat or woolly hat depending on the weather conditions.

✳ Shoes for when your little one wants to get out. Wellies are great for a puddle splashing break!

For you

✳ Appropriate shoes (check the guide at the start of the walk) and coat. Keep a light waterproof in the pram ready for emergencies.

✳ Food and drink: it's very easy to forget your own in the rush to pack your baby's feast!

✳ Mobile phone.

✳ Small first aid kit.

✳ This guidebook and the relevant Ordnance Survey map for the walk.

The Countryside Code

✳ Respect – Protect – Enjoy

✳ Do not drop litter. Use a bin or take it home.

✳ Do not stray from public footpaths or bridleways.

✳ Do not pick any plants.

✳ Make no unnecessary noise.

✳ Keep dogs on a lead near livestock and under close control at all other times.

✳ Leave gates as you find them.

✳ Use gates or stiles to cross fences, hedges or walls.

✳ Do not touch livestock, crops or farm machinery.

✳ Keep the natural water supply clean.

✳ Walk in single file and on the right-hand side of roads.

✳ Do not cross railway lines except by bridges.

✳ Guard against the risk of fire.

✳ For information on new access rights, visit www.countysideaccess.gov.uk or phone 0845 100 3298.

Why walk?

✳ Walking makes you feel good

✳ Walking reduces stress

✳ Walking helps you see more of your surroundings

✳ Walking helps you return to your pre-pregnancy figure and …

✳ Walking helps your baby learn about his/her surroundings and nature.

Circular route.

There and back. Route is non-circular.

Easy route with very few hills.

Moderate exertion. Some gentle ascents and descents.

Hard going. Route incorporates some steep inclines.

Easy terrain, trainers suitable.

Muddy and wet. Wellington boots or hiking boots are required.

Rough terrain. Rocky and uneven ground, hiking boots recommended.

Stile.

Icecream van on route!

Tea shop.

Pub/Hotel.

Picnic table.

Children's playground.

Ducks!

Toilets.

Solo. Walk can be accomplished alone.

At least two people required to complete walk. Pushchair may need to be lifted over obstacles.

Money required for parking, entrance fee or rail fare.

Walk 1: Birkett Common and Lammerside Castle

Allow: *2 hours*

This is a very pleasant walk along green lanes and bridleways. The tracks can be muddy in wet weather so make sure you are prepared! You will get great views of the River Eden and the opportunity to see the ruins of two castles.

Just down the road from the start point is Pendragon Castle, a 12th-century Norman Keep with 14th-century Garderobe turret. Pendragon Castle is reputed to be the castle of Uther Pendragon, father of King Arthur, but the present ruins are Norman and built by Henry II and later restored by Lady Anne Clifford. At the half-way point of the walk is the 12th-century Lammerside Castle. This second castle was rebuilt in the 14th century to provide protection against Scottish raiders. The castle was abandoned by the Wharton family in the 17th century when they moved to the nearby fortified manor house, Wharton Hall. All that remains now is part of the castle's central core.

Map: Ordnance Survey 1:25000 Explorer OL19 – grid reference 779029

Distance: 3½ miles

Getting there: Drive from Sedbergh along the A683 and take the turning on the right signposted to Outhgill and Mallerstang. Drive down this road until you see a signpost for a public byway to Wharton on the left-hand side just before a cattle grid. Park on the roadside here.

Walk down the byway which starts off as a gravel track with a dry stone wall on the right-hand side. The track soon turns to grass and can be wet in places.

> The hills to the right are High Pike and Bells and to the left is Birkett Common. As you walk along the track you will get views of the River Eden to the right and the ruins of Lammerside Castle ahead.

Pendragon Castle

Stay on this track as it bends to the left and passes over several fords and a small bridge. Eventually you will arrive at a gateway with Croop House ahead.

1. Follow the track from the gateway up to the houses ahead. Turn left and walk along the lane with the houses on your right.

   If you fancy a small diversion go through a second gateway on your right which takes you up to the ruins of Lammerside Castle.

2. Shortly after you have passed the houses bear right along a grass path. Don't stay on the main path which leads up to a gateway for Furrow Green. Go through a gateway which leads you onto a grass track in between two dry stone walls.

   After a slightly bumpy start this grass path smoothes out and leads you up through a further gateway and then underneath a railway bridge. Go through the gate at the far end of the bridge and follow the grass path straight ahead.

3. Simply stay on this track, avoiding any wet areas, until you reach a road (Tommy Road). Turn left and walk down this road all the way back to the start of the walk where you left your car.

In the area:

Crossbank Nature Reserve (www.fatlamb.co.uk). This is a wetland nature reserve behind The Fat Lamb Inn and Restaurant. Entry is free and there is a wheelchair accessible path which gives a good overall view of the site. Additional footpaths lead to viewpoints within the reserve.

Pendragon Castle. The ruins of this castle are just down the road from the walk start point and have open access all year round. It is thought to be the site of the castle of Uther Pendragon, father of King Arthur. The present ruins are Norman, built by Henry II and later restored by Lady Anne Clifford.

Walk 2: The Stang Forest Walk

Allow: *1 hour 15 minutes*

This is an easy, level walk around Forestry Commission coniferous forest. The tracks are broad and firm making ATP pushing very easy and great for large groups. If you are lucky you will see plenty of local wildlife including deer.

There are many tracks through this forest and I have chosen just a simple circular route. However, once you are familiar with the area it is worth returning and exploring the forest more extensively.

Map: Ordnance Survey 1:25000 Explorer OL30 – grid reference 023081

Distance: 2½ miles

Getting there: Park in the car park at the centre of the forest. This is on the left-hand side of the road as you are driving north, and opposite it is a metal barrier and gravel tracks into the forest on the other side of the road. Although it is possible to walk in the forest to the right of the road it is not always recommended as there are frequent shooting and rally driving events.

Leave the car park and turn left onto the road. Walk down the road (north), cross over Doorgill Bridge and then take the next turning on the left. This takes you to a fence with a low stile which you will have to lift the pushchair over.

1. Follow this grass and gravel track as it winds its way into the forest. Eventually this track will meet a broad gravel track. Turn left and follow this forestry track further into the woodland.

2. Continue straight ahead at the crossroads which is next to a pond. Follow the track as it bears round to the left and continues all the way back to the road.

3. Turn left onto the road and walk a short distance downhill back to the car park.

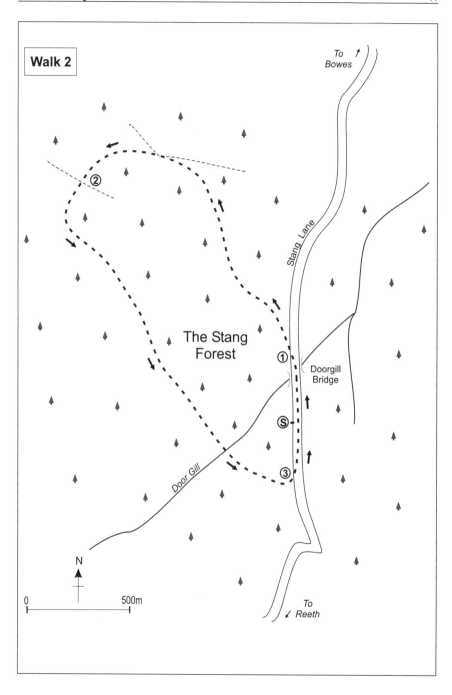

In the area:

Thorpe Farm Centre. A fun day out for all the family. A wooden play area, trampoline and popular pets corner. Also on site are a falconry centre, butchers, craft shop and coffee shop. Open seven days a week all year round.

(www.thorpefarm.co.uk; 01833 627242)

The Otter Trust, Bowes. This reserve is set in beautiful wild upland landscape and is a great place to take the kids for the day. There is a visitor's centre, tea shop and several breeding enclosures for the otters. There is also a model farm on site with sheep, goats, cattle and

View from Stang Forest

ponies. Open daily between 1st April and 31st October. (www.ottertrust.org.uk/pennines_home.html; 01833 628339)

Walk 3: Cautley Spout, Sedbergh

Allow: *1 hour 15 minutes or 2 hours*

Cautley Spout falls are a series of waterfalls which start from Cautley Crag on the side of the Calf, the highest of the Howgill peaks. They fall a total of 700ft and were formed when a glacier eroded into the mountainside diverting a stream over the edge of Cautley Crag. There is evidence of an Iron Age Settlement in the valley below the falls. A stone-edged path was found between the settlement and the falls suggesting that they held some significance for these people.

This walk can be done as a simple 'there and back' route to the falls or as a circular route incorporating both the falls and views of the Rawthey valley. The circular route crosses areas of moorland which can be boggy and, therefore, is only recommended in dry weather. However, the walk to the falls and back is accessible all year round.

Map: Ordnance Survey 1:25000 Explorer OL19 – grid reference 698969

Distance: 2¼ or 4 miles

Getting there: Park in the layby next to the Cross Keys Inn on the A683 between Sedbergh and Kirkby Stephen.

Take the footpath signposted to Cautley Spout from the layby. This takes you down a few steps and across a wooden footbridge over the River Rawthey. This bridge is very narrow so you may find it easier to carry the baby and the pram down separately and get set up for the walk on the other side (hence the recommendation for two people). Once over the bridge follow the gravel path as it bears to the left.

1. As the path turns to the right you will be able to see the waterfall, Cautley Spout, in the hills ahead of you. Continue along this path, passing a notice board with information on the falls and surrounding area.

Cautley Spout Falls

2. The path takes you all the way up to the base of the falls so you can walk as far as you want to. You will have to pass over a few tiny streams on the way and a couple of rocky areas. It is possible to walk up to the top of the falls but the track is very steep and so not recommended for pushchairs.

If you are doing the 'there and back' route then simply return along the same path.

If you are doing the circular route then return along the same path until you have passed the information board. Then shortly after this follow a faint path to the right which crosses a wooden foot-bridge over Cautley Holme Beck and then passes between two dry stone walls.

3. Go through the gateway and follow the path as it bears to the left through a second gateway, don't take the path straight ahead. Walk with a dry stone wall on your right and you will soon pass a barn and go through a third gateway.

Cross two fields and go through a small gateway with Cautley

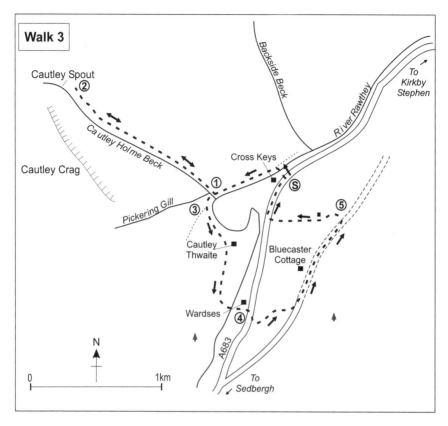

Thwaite Farm on your left. Follow the path straight ahead alongside the farm house. Go through another gateway and continue along the path with the fence on your left-hand side.

Pass a barn on your right and follow the path through the gate as it bears to the left. Cross a small stone bridge over the river and follow the track up to the road.

If you want to cut the walk short then turn left onto the road and follow it back to your car. This shortcut avoids the boggy moorland areas.

4. Cross the road and go up the bridleway signposted Hollow Lane. This path goes through a gateway and follows a gulley all the way up the field.

At the top of the hill go through the gate and turn left onto the lane. Pass through another gate and follow the lane up and past Bluecaster Cottage.

You will now have great views over the Rawthey valley with the Howgills over to your left. If you look down into the valley you will be able to see Cautley Spout again.

5. Once you have past the cottage, continue up the track and pass the last fence on your left. Look out for a very faint grass path on the left across the moorland about 100m after the fence.

Follow this path down as it curves to the left, keep a look out as the path is very faint. The path takes you down and through a gateway to the left of a small barn. Continue along the path as it heads down through a further gate and winds its way down the hill to a final gateway onto the road.

Turn right and follow the road a short distance to the Cross Keys Inn and your car.

The Inn serves food and also has a small shop at the back of the building where you can buy refreshments.

In the area:

Queen's Gardens, Sedbergh. A forgotten Victorian park with wheel-chair accessible paths to the west of Sedbergh on the A684 towards Kendal. The garden is managed as a wildlife habitat making it a great place to spot insects and birds.

Farfield Mill Arts and Heritage Centre, Sedbergh. This old woollen mill was in production for 156 years between 1836-1992. The restored mill now houses a number of exhibitions from local and national artists. There is a shop, café and toilets on site. Check online for opening times(www.farfieldmill.org; 015396 21958).

Walk 4: Shaw Paddock to Hellgill

Allow: 1 hour 45 minutes

A fantastic walk along green lanes giving great views of both the Eden and Ure Valleys. The route takes you through outstanding scenery almost to the source of the River Ure on Lunds Fell. The first section of the walk can be muddy and boggy in sections but the rest of the route is on good even lanes and quiet roads.

Features of this walk are the impressive 26ft waterfall, Hell Gill Force and Hell Gill Bridge. This bridge has a single arch and dates from 1825 replacing a much more ancient construction. The bridge is located on a bridleway known as the Lady Anne Highway. Lady Anne Clifford was a renowned noblewoman of the Stuart era who was born at Skipton Castle in 1590. She spent much of her life restoring churches and castles (e.g. Skipton, Pendragon and Brougham) and this path is the route that she took between her many castles and estates.

Map: Ordnance Survey 1:25000 Explorer OL19 – grid reference 785951

Distance: 3 miles

Getting there: Park on the road-side next to Shaw Paddock Farm just before a railway bridge on the B6259.

Walk towards the railway bridge (north) and you will see a sign-posted track (Bridleway to Hell Gill Bridge 1 mile) that takes you through the farm yard. The gravel track takes you over the River Ure at How Beck Bridge. After the bridge the track turns from gravel to grass and can be boggy in wet weather.

There are great views of Swarth Fell, Wild Boar Fell and Mallerstang Common to your left and Lunds Fell to the right.

1. When you come to a fork in the grass track take the right-hand path and follow it as it heads gently uphill. The path takes you up

to the right of some rocky outcrops where there is a cave. At the top of the path turn left onto a stony track (Lady Anne Highway). Walk along this track to Hell Gill Bridge crossing a ford on the way.

Look over the right-hand wall of the bridge and you will see the stream, Hell Gill Beck, running down a deep ravine.

Hellgill Force

2. Go through the gate at the end of the bridge and then turn immediately left through another gateway marked as a footpath. This grass track takes you down to Hellgill Farm. Pass the house on your right, go through a gateway and then follow the track to a further gateway.

3. Soon you will cross a second bridge over Hell Gill Beck and the path then takes you down to a T-junction. Turn left here and follow the path over a railway bridge, through a gateway and up to the road (B6259).

Hell Gill Force is just a short detour from the t-junction. Go straight ahead on the faint grass path and follow this for about 10m and you will see this impressive waterfall on your right.

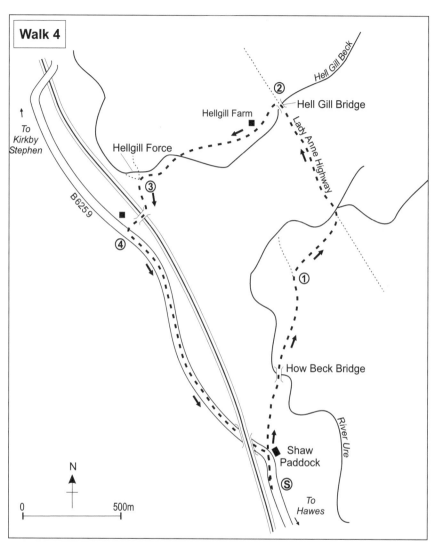

Turn left and follow the road back to your car, watching out for traffic.

In the area:

Hardraw Force (www.hardrawforce.com; 01969 667572). This is the largest single drop waterfall in England. Entry is through the historic Green Dragon Inn and it is possible to take a pleasant walk through the grounds as well as up to this impressive 100ft waterfall. There are picnic tables within the grounds and refreshments are also served in the pub.

The Buttertubs are a series of dramatic shallow potholes that can be seen on the eastern side of Shunner Fell. The formations are on the roadside along the Thwaite to Hawes Road (Buttertubs Pass) approximately 2½ miles south of Thwaite. There is a small car park and information board next to the formations.

Walk 5: Muker Side and Cliff Beck

Allow: *1 hour 30 minutes*

Muker is a traditional dales village with Viking origins. The village name arose from the Norse word 'Mjor aker' meaning small piece of farmed land. However, Neolithic flint artefacts have been found in the area suggesting it was inhabited long before the Vikings arrived. Muker is now an area of international importance due to its flower rich hay meadows which are carefully protected. Farmers are given grants to allow them to use traditional farming methods free from artificial fertilizers in order to protect these sites.

The village has plenty to offer walkers. As well as great routes through beautiful dales scenery there are tea shop and pub refreshments and craft shops to browse. Although it is possible to complete this walk in all seasons parts of the route can be wet and muddy after wet weather. Therefore, it is best undertaken during the summer months.

Map: Ordnance Survey 1:25000 Explorer OL30 – grid reference 910978

Distance: 2½ miles

Getting there: Park in the pay and display car park next to the bridge in Muker.

Exit the car park with the bridge on your left and walk up the stony track to the right of the road signposted as a bridleway to Occupation Road.

> Below you to the left is Straw Beck which shortly runs into the River Swale. You will soon be rewarded with great views over Swaledale.

Follow the track up, through a gateway and continue along between two dry stone walls. The track soon crosses a small ford, bends to the right and begins a steady uphill climb.

Muker is now down to your right. The hill to the left of Muker is Kisdon and the one to the right is Black Hill.

As you get to the top of the hill the path levels out and you will see a track that heads off to the left. Ignore this and continue on the track straight ahead.

1. Cross the bridge over Greenseat Beck and then turn immediately right, down a grass and dirt track in between two dry stone walls. This part of the walk can be muddy in wet weather.

Muker Side and Kisdon Hill

2. When you reach a small barn and the track bends to the right, turn left through a gateway and follow the track with the dry stone wall on your right.

   Cross a small ford over Coal Sike and then follow the track between two dry stone walls. Go through another gateway and follow the wall to your right. You will pass some derelict buildings (Appletree Thwaite) on your right. The track then continues through a further two gateways.

3. After the second gateway follow the track as it crosses to the far left-hand corner of the field. Go through a gateway and turn immediately right and, if the water is low enough, cross the ford

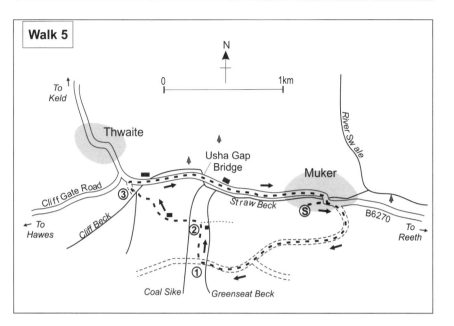

over Cliff Beck. If the water is too high there is a gap stile in the wall to the right of the gate within the field. Lift the pushchair over this, cross the narrow stone bridge and lift the pushchair over the gate on the other side. Whichever route you chose simply rejoin the track on the other side of the stream and follow it down to the road.

There is a small waterfall just below the ford.

Turn right onto the road (B6270) and simply follow it all the way back to Muker. This is a quiet road with a wide verge allowing you to get out of the way of any traffic.

If you are walking with a group and wish to avoid the road section then there is room to leave a second car close to where this track meets the road.

As you walk through Muker you will see several shops, toilets, the Farmers Arms Pub and a tea shop. Stay on this road with Cross Beck on your right, cross the bridge and find your car in the car park.

In the area:

Hazel Brow Farm (www.hazelbrow.co.uk; 01748 886224). This award winning organic farm is a great experience for all ages. There are animals to cuddle and feed, pony rides, traditional craft activities and graded walks around the farm. The farm is open from 30th March to 30th September between 11.00am to 6.00pm but is closed on Mondays and Fridays.

Swaledale Folk Museum, Reeth (01748 884118). This museum is based in the Old Merchant School and is a treasure house with over 500 objects connected with life and work in this dale. Open between Easter Monday and the beginning of September on Thursdays, Fridays and Sundays.

Walk 6: River Swale, Grinton

Allow: *2 hours*

A delightful riverside ramble along the banks of the River Swale. The route also follows part of the Yorkshire Dales Cycle Way and gives great views across the river and along the length of Swaledale. Swaledale is one of the wildest of the Yorkshire dales with England's fastest flowing river, the River Swale, running through it. Parts of the riverside path are at risk of flooding in extreme wet weather and the route would be inaccessible at this time.

Grinton was once an important crossing point on the river and the centre of an ancient parish belonging to Bridlington Priory. All that remains of this important history are the stone bridge and St Andrew's Church. The church is known as the cathedral of the dales and parts of it date back to the 12th century.

Map: Ordnance Survey 1:25000 Explorer OL30 – grid reference 020982

Distance: 3¾ miles

Getting there: When driving into Grinton on the B6270 turn left towards Redmire and Leyburn then immediately right up Swale Hall Lane signposted to Harkerside. Follow this road over a cattle grid and park in the small gravel area next to a bridleway signposted towards Castle Bolton via Whitaside.

Leave your car, turn left and walk down the road with the River Swale on your right.

> On the lower of the hills to your left is Maiden Castle. These are the remains of what is thought to be an Iron Age hillfort.

1. Walk down the road until you see a bridleway on your right signposted to Grinton 2¼ miles. Follow this grass path through a gateway and across a field. Go through a second gateway and continue along the path with the dry stone wall on your right. For

Footbridge over the River Swale

easiest walking stay close to the wall as the field slopes steeply down to the left.

The River Swale is now on your left. The village on the other side of the river is Healaugh.

The path then bears steeply down to the left, through a gateway and continues straight ahead following the river bank. There is a short section of cobbled path and it can be narrow in places. There is also an awkward tree root here which may necessitate lifting the pushchair.

Continue through a further gateway and you will soon be able to see a second grass track on your immediate right. Cut down onto this path and follow it across the field away from the river. Go through the gateway at the far corner of the field and turn left onto a stone track with a dry stone wall on your left.

You will see a footbridge over the river on your left which leads to a footpath to Reeth.

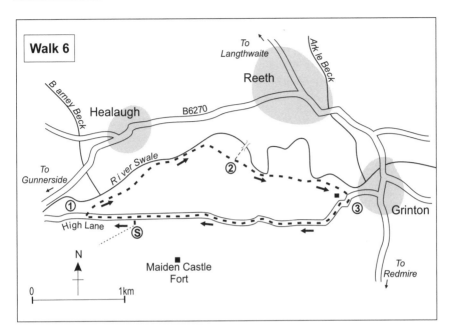

2. Continue on the grass path straight ahead; don't take the gravel track to the footbridge. Follow this path through four more gateways and you will then be back on the riverside path.

3. At the next gateway turn right and walk up the road passing Swale Hall on your right. This first section of road is quite steep but after 10 minutes or so it levels out. Follow this road past a cattle grid and all the way back to your car.

There are great views of Swaledale from this road. The town on your right is Reeth and behind this are Cuckoo Hill and Fremington Edge.

In the area:

Reeth Bakery and Tea Room (www.reethbakery.co.uk; 01748 884735). If you fancy some traditional pies and cakes for the walk or a snack once you are done then visit this bakery in Reeth. All food is handmade using traditional recipes and is delicious.

Richmond Castle (www.english-heritage.org.uk; 01748 822493). The castle is dramatically situated high on a rocky promontory and overlooks the River Swale. It was originally built by the Normans to control the North. Look round the castle and walk round the heritage garden. Open daily between March and September and every day except Tuesday and Wednesday for the rest of the year.

Walk 7: Clints Wood and Telfit Bank, Marske

Allow: *1 hour 30 minutes or 2 hours 45 minutes*

This is a great walk which takes you through woodland and across wild moors. There are fantastic views of limestone crags, a waterfall on the picturesque Marske Beck and across Swaledale. Marske was the birthplace of the Hutton family, the only English family to have yielded two archbishops. The Huttons built Marske Hall just to the south of the main village and great views of this building can be seen from its entrance gates.

There are two options for this walk. The full walk takes you up Telfit Bank and gives fantastic views across Swaledale. However, this does involve a long uphill push and there are some bumpy patches. The hill is quite exposed so if you chose this route make sure you take plenty of warm clothing for both you and the baby. The shorter walk is much easier going but does miss out some great views.

Map: Ordnance Survey 1:25000 Explorer OL30 – grid reference 104006

Distance: 3 miles or 5 miles

Getting there: Drive along the A6108 between Richmond and Leyburn and take the signposted turning for Marske which takes you down Cat Bank. Pass Marske Hall on your left and take the next turning on the right which takes you into the centre of the village. Turn left, just before the telephone box, up Cordilleras Lane. The walk starts from the 'no through road' almost immediately on your left. So park anywhere that you can find space within the village.

Walk along the 'no through road', passing the houses on your right. Pass through the gateway and follow the gravel track ahead, signposted as a public bridleway.

There are great views of this area of Swaledale throughout this

Clints Scar and Telfit Bank

walk. The stream to your left is Marske Beck and the woodland on the right is Clints Wood.

Follow this track passing over a cattle grid, through the small cluster of houses at Clints and into Clints Wood. After a while you will come to a fork in the track within the Wood. Turn left off the main track following the bridleway arrow and you will shortly come to a gateway. Go through the gateway and follow the grass track out of the woodland.

The limestone crag to your right is Clints Scar and below this is Limekiln Wood.

1. Follow the track through another gateway up to Orgate Farm. Take the concrete track on the left immediately before the farm and follow this down, over the beck and through another gateway.

   Look upstream when you cross Marske Beck and you will be able to see the waterfall Orgate Force.

2. The track takes you to a road, Skelton Lane. You now have a choice.

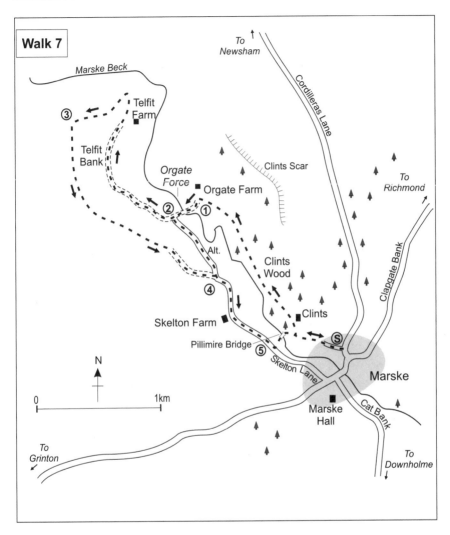

Walk 7

To Newsham

Marske Beck

Cordilleras Lane

Telfit Farm

③

Telfit Bank

Clints Scar

Orgate Force

Orgate Farm

To Richmond

② ①

Alt.

Clints Wood

④

Clints

Claggate Bank

Skelton Farm

Clints

Pillimire Bridge ⑤

Skelton Lane

Ⓢ

Marske

N

0   1km

Marske Hall

Cat Bank

To Grinton

To Downholme

To do the full walk, which takes you up and across Telfit Bank (the hill directly in front of you), turn right up the gravel track and follow the directions below. This route is slightly bumpy in places and is best avoided with very small babies.

To avoid the hill, turn left and follow the road back towards Marske. Follow the instructions from *** (point 5).

Follow this gravel track all the way to Telfit Farm passing through a gate along the way. Turn left immediately before the farm and follow the track through the gateway and up the hill.

At the first corner of this uphill track you will be able to see the rocky cliff, Dicky Edge ahead. Opposite this is Helwith Bank.

The track bears left and continues up hill to another gateway. Bumpy areas can usually be avoided by walking alongside the track. Go straight up through the grass field to another gateway. Shortly after this you will come to a crossroads where you turn left onto the gravel track. The track then levels out and it is easy going from then on.

3. Follow this grass track all the way along the top of the hill, passing through a gateway along the way. Go through another gateway and follow the path between two stone walls down into the valley.

4. The track takes you down to Skelton Lane. Turn right and follow the lane towards Marske.

5. *** Soon after you pass a house on the left you will see a gateway on the left that takes you onto a public footpath. This crosses a field and takes you down to Marske Beck. Cross over the stone bridge (Pillimire Bridge), go through the gateway and follow the grass track that goes straight up the bank ahead. This brings you back to the gravel track we followed at the beginning of the walk. Turn right and follow the track back to you car.

In the area:

Constable Burton Hall Gardens. These beautiful gardens offer both woodland walks and garden trails. The gardens are open between March and October and garden and house tours are available by appointment. (www.constableburtongardens.co.uk; 01677 460225)

Easby Abbey. The substantial ruins of this medieval abbey stand near to the River Swale near Richmond. The ruins can be reached via road or a pleasant walk from Richmond Castle (see walk 6). Open daily all year (www.english-heritage.org.uk).

Walk 8: Flinter Gill, Dent

Allow: *2 hours 30 minutes*

This is the hardest walk in this book but for those tough enough to attempt it the rewards are great. The views over Dentdale, Deepdale and the Howgills are spectacular on a clear day. The walk begins with a long steep rocky uphill climb and for this reason I have recommended it be attempted by two people so you can take turns pushing. After crossing a high moorland path the route takes a steep and very rocky downhill track back into the valley. It is possible to avoid this rocky downhill path by simply returning along the route you came. Although the walk can be done all year round it can be very muddy and wet and so is best undertaken during the summer.

Dent is one of the prettiest and most distinct villages in the Yorkshire Dales with its cobbled streets and whitewashed cottages. It is the only village in Dentdale that was inhabited by Norse settlers, who preferred to live in isolated farmhouses. Dent was the birthplace of Adam Sedgwick (1785-1873) the father of British geology and was also renowned for its 'terrible knitters'. These knitters were so called as they were terribly good and were known for their speed and accuracy.

Map: Ordnance Survey 1:25000 Explorer OL2 – grid reference 704871

Distance: 4½ miles

Getting there: Park in the pay and display car park in the village of Dent. There are picnic tables and toilets here.

Leave the car park, go straight across the road and up a lane alongside Dent Memorial Hall, signposted to Dragon Croft. Pass a children's playground on your left and instead of following the road round to the left go up a 'no through road' straight ahead, signposted to Flinter Gill.

Dent village

1. Follow this as it becomes a stony track and heads steeply uphill following alongside the stream Flinter Gill and passing through three gateways along the way. At the top of the track there is a bench for a much needed rest.

2. Go through another gateway and then turn left onto a broad track (Green Lane). The track crosses Flinter Gill and bends to the left.

   Look behind you and you will see the Howgills. Down below you to the left is Dentdale and Deepdale will gradually come into view up ahead.

3. Stay on the track until you come to a junction where you turn left through a gateway signposted as a bridleway to Nun House Outrake 1 mile. This track is extremely rocky and can be avoided by returning along the route you came. Follow this track down through another gateway and back down into Dentdale.

   This stony track takes you down to a road (Deepdale Lane). Turn left, passing Peacock Hill Farm and follow the road down hill.

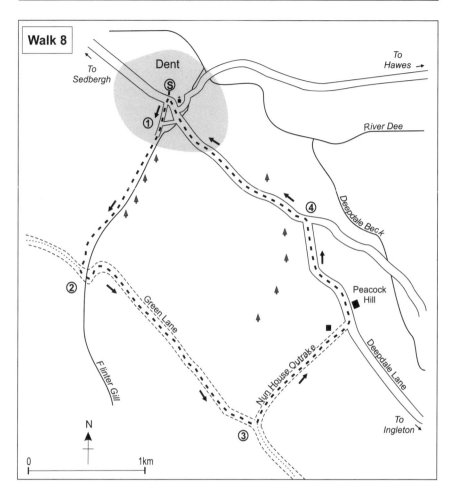

After a while you will come to a junction where you turn left following the signs for Dent.

4. This road takes you all the way back into Dent. Walk through the village along the cobbled streets and when you get to the George and Dragon Inn continue straight ahead, don't turn right. The road winds its way back to the car park passing the Sun Inn and the tea shop along the way.

In the area:

Holme Open Farm (015396 20654). Go on one of the nature trails or enjoy a riverside picnic. Farm tours allow you to touch, hold and feed the baby animals and there are seasonal demonstrations. The farm is open daily between March and September.

Dent Crafts Centre (015396 25400). A wide range of local crafts are on display in the gallery and once you have had a look why not enjoy some refreshments in the tearoom. The centre is open six days a week (closed Tuesdays) between Easter and November.

Walk 9: Cam High Road to Wether Fell

Allow: *1 hour 30 minutes*

Pick a clear day for this simple walk along an ancient Roman road and you will be rewarded with the most spectacular views over the full length of Wensleydale. You will get a clear view of Semer Water, Yorkshire's only natural lake which is surrounded by myths and legends. The route passes alongside the top of Wether Fell, the 29th highest peak in the Dales at 614m (just over 2000 ft). Bear in mind that this is a high level walk and the track can be quite exposed, so don't forget hats and woollies.

The walk follows Cam High Road, a Roman Road thought to have been built around AD80. At this time Agricola, the most successful of the governors of Britain, built a fort for a permanent garrison at Brough Hill, Bainbridge. A number of roads were built to support this fort and Cam High is one of the two that remain to the present day. This road was thought to go all the way to Ribchester but now only goes as far as Ingleton.

Map: Ordnance Survey 1:25000 Explorer OL30 – grid reference 862853

Distance: 3¼ miles

Getting there: From Hawes drive in the direction of Gayle and Kettlewell. There is space for roadside parking on the top of the steep hill on Beggarmans Road.

The walk begins at the very top of the steep hill were a broad stone and gravel track leaves the road (signposted as a Byway to Bainbridge). This is Cam High Road. The track follows a stone wall to the right for the first 10 minutes and then is intermittently bordered by two stone walls.

There are fantastic views of Dodd Fell and the surrounding dales to the left.

1. After approximately 25 minutes of easy climbing you will reach the highest point in the track and on your immediate left is Wether Fell. It is only a short walk to the top of the fell from here but the path is not suitable for pushchairs.

Over the wall to your right you will be able to see Semer Water (the largest natural water body in the Dales) and beyond that the distinctive peak of Addlebrough.

Cam High Road

2. Simply stay on this main track until you reach a gateway. This is the turning point for the walk so turn around and follow the track back to your car. It is possible to continue along this track all the way to Bainbridge. However, it is a long downhill and unless you go with a group and park a car at either end it isn't to be recommended.

This is a popular area for Para gliders so look out for them in the skies above Wether Fell and Yorburgh.

In the area:

Wensleydale Creameries (www.wensleydale.co.uk; 01969 667664). See the making of traditional Wensleydale cheese, follow

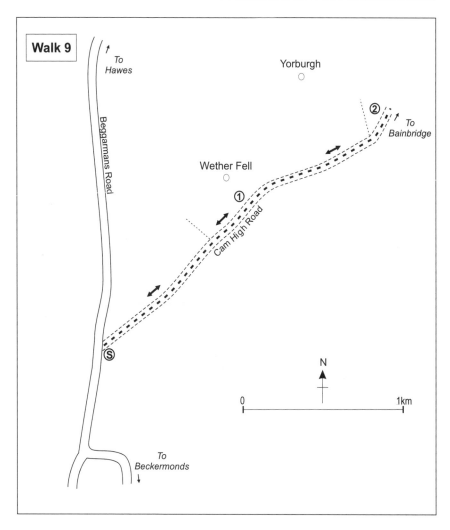

the museum tour and taste the range of cheeses made here. There is also a restaurant and coffee shop. Open daily, however, cheese isn't made every day so phone ahead if you want to see this.

Dales Countryside Museum (www.destinationdales.org.uk; 01969 667450). Discover the lives of people past and present in the Yorkshire Dales. There are demonstrations, videos, workshops and a shop. Open daily 10.00am to 5.00pm.

Walk 10: Aysgarth Falls

Allow: 1 hour

This is an extremely beautiful and easy walk which takes you to see a series of three waterfalls on the River Ure, with an extra detour through Freeholders' Wood Nature Reserve. Aysgarth falls are some of the most dramatic waterfalls in the Yorkshire Dales and consequently one of the most visited locations. The falls have formed due to an alternation of near-horizontal layers of hard limestone and soft shale. The water has cut back into the shale and undercut the limestone layers. Limestone blocks have broken off leaving the waterfalls that we see today.

Freeholders' Wood is an ancient woodland which has had tree cover since at least 1600. The woodland contains several native tree species and is home to many wild mammals and birds. The woodland is especially beautiful in spring when the wild flowers come into bloom.

Map: Ordnance Survey 1:25000 Explorer OL30 – grid reference 011887

Distance: 2 miles

Getting there: Park in the National Park car park at Aysgarth Falls, Church Bank, Aysgarth. There is a fee for parking. There is a National Park Information Centre and shop at the car park. The café sells hot and cold food and ice cream and has highchairs and bibs. The toilets have baby-changing facilities.

When you leave the visitor's centre turn left and follow the signs for the upper falls. As you follow this tarmac path along you will soon see the road and a bridge on the left. Go through the gateway ahead when you reach the road.

1. Go through a small gateway to the left which takes you straight to the upper falls and a picnic area. Once you have seen the falls follow the path back to the visitor's centre.

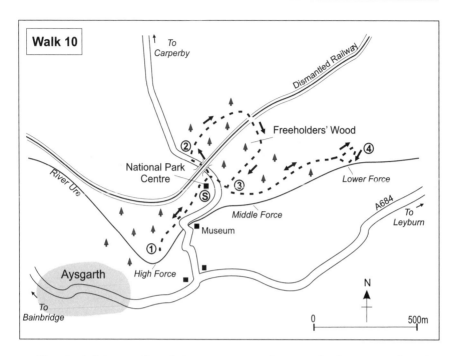

Go straight past the visitor centre and towards the car park exit. Do not follow the fenced path to the right here which leads to the middle and lower falls. Turn left onto the road and go under the bridge. As you walk up the road you will pass a lane up to the old railway station on your right. Pass a small gate leading to a foot-path to Carperby Village on your right.

2. Then take the next footpath on the right, through a large gate in the direction of Castle Bolton. Follow this woodland track to two junctions in series. Go straight ahead at both of these, not to the right or left respectively. At the next junction take the right fork which soon leads you down through the stone buttresses of an old railway bridge. Go over a short section of boardwalk and then continue on the woodland path.

   Turn right at the crossroads. This is a woodland path so there is the occasional tree root or stone but on the whole the path is very good.

Lower Falls, Aysgarth

3. The path brings you to a junction with a gate to the road on the right. Turn left here following the signs to the middle and lower falls. You will soon come to a series of steps down to the middle falls view point. There is a bench at the top of these steps that gives you a great view but if you have time it is worth going down to the view point. It's easiest to leave the pushchair at the top.

To go to the lower falls, continue along the path through the woodland. Go through a gateway and then shortly after this you will see a gateway on your right marked as 'riverside return path'. Ignore this and continue straight ahead. There is a long series of concrete steps to go down but it is definitely worth it once you get down to the falls.

4. Push the pushchair over the rocky shore and go up the return path which begins with a few small steps. This then takes you up a woodland path to the gateway off the main path you passed earlier. Turn left and follow this track back past the middle falls. You will come to a fork in the path with gateways at the end of both paths. Take the right fork, go through the gateway, cross the road and follow the path back to the visitor's centre.

In the area:

Black Sheep Brewery, Masham (www.blacksheepbrewery.com; 01765 680100). This is a great place for all the family. Be shepherded round the brewery tour and see how the beers are made. Sample the beers and stop for a meal in the restaurant. Check opening times online.

The Teapottery, Leyburn (www.teapottery.co.uk; 01969 623839). The largest collection of crazy teapots in England. Tour the pottery and watch the teapots being cast, moulded and painted. Enjoy a cuppa and a cake in the tea room. Admission free and open daily.

Walk 11: Bolton Hall, Wensley

Allow: 1 hour 30 minutes

An easy walk on flat tracks through the beautiful parkland of Bolton Hall Estate. The walk begins in the pretty village of Wensley which gives this Yorkshire dale its name. Wensley was once an important market town until the plague wiped out its inhabitants. The village has a 13th-century church and a restored water mill where candles are now made.

Bolton Hall was built in 1678 by Charles Powlett to replace Bolton Castle. It was partially rebuilt in 1902 after a serious fire. The house is now the residence of the current Lord Bolton and is not open to the public. However, this walk gives you great views of the grounds and takes you right past the front of the house. The turning point for this walk is Lords Bridge which spans the River Ure. This is a beautiful spot for a picnic so make sure you go equipped!

Map: Ordnance Survey 1:25000 Explorer OL30 – grid reference 091896

Distance: 3 miles

Getting there: Drive into Wensley on the A684 from Leyburn, pass the Three Horseshoes pub on your left and take the next turning on the right. Park here next to the village green.

Walk through the stone gateway and follow this road all the way to Bolton Hall. This is a no-through road for Bolton Hall Estate only. The road has two cattle grids on route, both with gates on the right. Simply go through these and continue to follow the road ahead.

> There are great views over Wensleydale with West Witton Moor and Penhill on your left.

As you pass an area of coniferous planting on the right you will begin to see glimpses of Bolton Hall ahead. You will then come to a fork, take the left fork towards Bolton Farm.

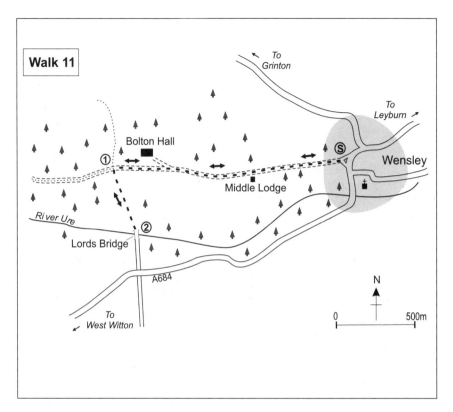

1. Once you have passed the house you will come to a crossroads. Turn left through the gateway and follow the track all the way through the field to Lords Bridge.

   If you want to extend the walk you can go straight ahead at the crossroads and follow the track as it goes past open pasture and woodland (West Wood). When you are ready, turn back and follow the same track back.

2. Lords Bridge is the turning point for this walk. The bridge spans the River Ure and the banks of the river make a tranquil spot for a picnic. There are also great views back over Bolton Hall from here.

   Return to your car by the same route.

Bolton Hall

In the area:

Bolton Castle (www.boltoncastle.co.uk; 01969 623981). This massive fortress has dominated Wensleydale since 1379 and is one of England's best preserved castles. View the Royal Bedchambers, Dungeons and the castle gardens. There are tea rooms in the 14th-century guest hall or you can take a picnic to eat in the grounds.

Beech End Model Village (www.beech-end.co.uk; 01969 625400). This model village is interactive and provides indoor entertainment for all the family. It is possible to drive vehicles through the village and to hear the sounds within the shops and houses. Beech End is open between March and October but check the website or phone ahead for opening times.

Walk 12: Jervaulx Abbey and Park

Allow: *1 hour 15 minutes*

Set in sheep grazing parkland, Jervaulx Abbey is a dramatic site. The Abbey was a Cistercian house established in 1156. The ruins are a reminder of Henry VIII's determination to destroy the power of monasteries. In 1536 the Pilgrimage of Grace began from Jervaulx in the hope of persuading the King against this destruction. Once the monks had returned to the dales the King imprisoned and executed the pilgrimage leader, Abbot Adam Sedburgh, and destroyed Jervaulx.

The walk takes you for a leisurely stroll past the abbey ruins and through the parkland. This is a wonderful walk for a summer's day and there is plenty of opportunity for a picnic. There is also the option of tea and ice creams in the Abbey Tearooms.

Map: Ordnance Survey 1:25000 Explorer 302 – grid reference 168856

Distance: 2¼ miles

Getting there: Park in the Jervaulx Abbey and Tea Rooms car park. There is an honesty box here where you can pay the small parking fee.

Walk to the entrance of the car park. Cross the road and go through the metal gates into the abbey grounds.

1. After just a couple of minutes you will come to a crossroads in the path. Take the path to the right, not straight ahead to the abbey. Simply follow this broad stony track through Jervaulx Park for about 30 minutes.

   As you walk along you can see the abbey on your left which is surrounded by grassland and grazing sheep. You will then pass a farmhouse on the right and a small pond on the left. There are plenty of places to stop for a picnic along the route.

Jervaulx Abbey

2. Eventually you will come to the gates at the end of the track with a house on the left. Go through the right-hand gate and this brings you to a quiet country lane (Kilgram Lane). Turn right and follow the lane for approximately 15 minutes taking care for traffic.

3. The lane takes you to the main road (A6108). As you walk up to the junction you will see a house on the right. Turn right immediately after the house and go through the gate into the field following signs for the public footpath.

Once you are in the field you will see a group of trees on your left. Walk just to the right of these trees and follow the faint track through the parkland. You are now back in Jervaulx Park. After 10 minutes you will come to a junction in the track with the pond you passed earlier on your right. Turn left and follow the track back to the abbey.

Soon you will see the abbey on your right. When you get to the crossroads next to the abbey, turn left and go through the gates. Cross the road and find your car in the car park.

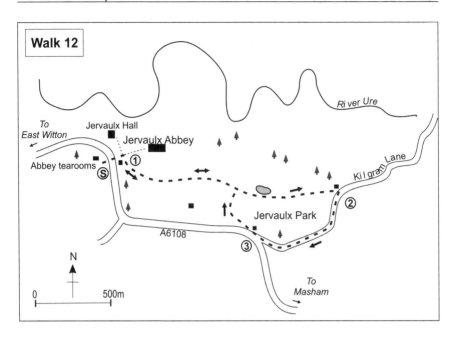

If you want some refreshments before you leave, pop into the Abbey tearooms where you can pick up snacks or stop to eat. There are also a gift shop, garden shop and toilets here.

In the area:

Brymor Ice Cream (www.brymordairy.co.uk; 01677 460377). Try some real Yorkshire Dales ice cream made from milk from their own herd of Guernsey cattle, and double cream. There are thirty five flavours to try as well as frozen yoghurt and sorbet. They also sell traditional cheeses, clotted cream and cartons of ice cream for those who want to take some away. Toilets with baby changing facilities. Open daily 10.00am-6.00pm.

Thorp Perrow Arboretum, Woodland Garden and Falconry Centre (www.thorpperrow.com; 01677 425323). This 85-acre arboretum is one of the finest private collections of trees and shrubs in the country. Created by Colonel Sir Leonard Ropner (1895-1977) this wonderful garden is perfect for a tranquil walk any time of year. There is a nature trail, a children's trail, lake, picnic area, children's play area and tea rooms. Open all year from dawn to dusk.

Walk 13: Chapel-le-Dale, Ingleton

Allow: 1 hour 45 minutes

This is a great all-weather walk along farm tracks and minor roads with fantastic views all the way. You will be able to see two of the three peaks, Whernside and Ingleborough, which dominate the local skyline. This walk also affords great views of the spectacular Ribblehead Viaduct and, if you are lucky, you may see a steam train crossing it.

Ribblehead Viaduct was built in 1876 and has a 24-arch span. It was built in five years by hundreds of navvies who lived in a camp at Ribblehead. There are many tales of horrific accidents and disease during the building of the viaduct and Blea Moor Tunnel. Nobody knows how many men died but there is a memorial to them within St Leonard's Church, Chapel-le-Dale.

Map: Ordnance Survey 1:25000 Explorer OL2 – grid reference 735770

Distance: 3¾ miles

Getting there: Drive along the B6255 between Ingleton and Ribblehead and take the small turning signposted to Chapel-le-Dale church near the Hill Inn. Follow the road round to the left until you pass over a cattle grid. Park on the grass immediately after this.

Walk back along the road, over the cattle grid and towards St Leonard's church. Turn left immediately before the church and follow the road up and over a cattle grid.

> The cave Hurtle Pot is on the right straight after the church. It is reputed to be the home of a Boggard, a Dales sprite!

1. At the fork in the track turn right up a stony track towards Gill Head and Ellerbeck.

> You will shortly pass a sculpture on the left by Charles l'Anson.

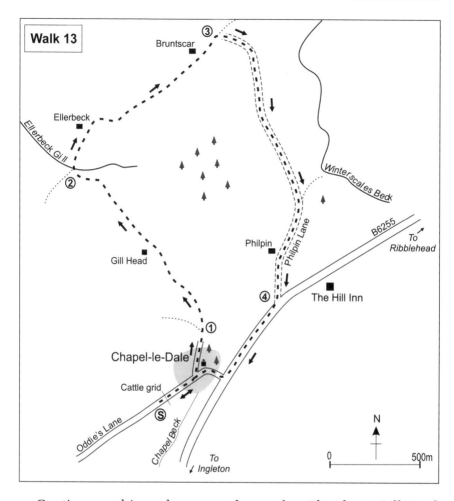

Continue up this track over another cattle grid and past Gill Head on the left.

Soon you will have great views of Whernside ahead and Ingleborough behind you. As you near the top of this track Ribblehead Viaduct will come into view on your right.

2. At the next junction turn right following the track towards Deepdale. Depending on recent weather there may be a ford crossing Ellerbeck Gill at this junction.

Go straight over the cattle grid and up to an old farm house. Pass through the gateway and follow the path past the house and through the farmyard. This brings you down to a wooden gate on the right with a bridleway signpost. Follow this track over another cattle grid and continue until you come to some more houses at Bruntscar.

Statue by Charles l'Anson

3. Take the next turning on the right down a tarmac road signposted to the Hill Inn. Pass over another cattle grid and follow this road all the way down until you reach the B6255.

On your way down you will pass a farm at Philpin where there is a snack bar and toilet. This is open at weekends between the end of April and October.

4. Turn right onto the road and stay on the right-hand side where there is a verge with enough room for you to escape any traffic.

If you fancy some refreshments the Hill Inn is just up the road, serves great food and has a highchair.

Continue down the road for about five minutes and turn right down the turning for Chapel-le-Dale church. Bear left at the church and you will find your car straight after the cattle grid.

In the area:

Ingleton Waterfalls Walk (www.ingletonwaterfallswalk.co.uk; 01756 795621). This walk was first opened in 1885 and has some of the most spectacular waterfall and woodland scenery in the north of England. The walk covers 4½ miles and takes between 2½-4 hours to complete. There are lots of steps so this is not pushchair friendly so take a child carrier instead. Open daily 9.00am till dusk.

White Scar Cave, Ingleton (www.whitescarcave.co.uk; 01524 241244). This is the longest show cave in Britain and has gushing streams, waterfalls and exotic cave formations. There is an 80-minute tour that covers 1 mile and takes you into the massive 330ft Battlefield Cavern. There are picnic grounds with views over Chapel-le-Dale and a café and shop. Open daily from 10.00am between February and October and at weekends between November and January.

Walk 14: Buckden Rake

Allow: 1 hour 45 minutes

Buckden Rake is part of an old Roman road that ran between Ilkley (Olicana) and Bainbridge (Virosidum). This wonderful track heads up from the village and across the lower flanks of the hill, Buckden Pike. Once the initial climb is over the path levels out and gives excellent views over Langstrothdale.

In the 12th century, Langstrothdale was home to the main hunting lodge of the Earl of Northumberland. Buckden was founded as an administrative centre to look after this hunting forest. Little remains of the woodland but this beautiful area is now a very popular walking destination.

Waterfall at the side of Buckden Rake

Map: Ordnance Survey 1:25000 Explorer OL30 – grid reference 942773

Distance: 3¼ miles

Getting there: Park in the National Park pay and display car park in Buckden. There are toilets here but no baby changing facilities. There is also a grassy area in the car park with benches.

Walk to the far end of the car park, through a gate onto an uphill track signposted to Buckden Pike and Cray High Bridge. Continue along this track over several short rocky sections as it heads up the hill.

Look behind you for great views over Buckden. Down to your right you will be able to see the River Wharfe winding its way through the valley.

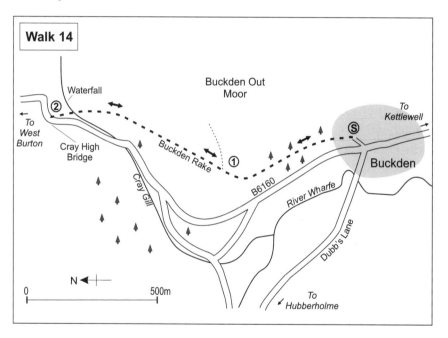

1. After a good half an hour uphill climb, go through a gateway and continue on the path ahead. Once you are at the top of the hill take the left-hand fork in the path which leads you through another gateway onto a grassy track signposted for Cray High Bridge. Simply continue along this path passing through a number of gateways.

This track is called Buckden Rake and is an old Roman Road. Up to your right is Buckden Pike and over to your left is Chapel Moor. As you walk along you will see the village of Cray down on the left and the White Lion Inn. This can be reached by heading down the road towards Buckden from Cray High Bridge.

2. Towards the end of the track you will go through a couple of fords and pass a lovely waterfall on your right. Finally you will reach the turning point for the walk, a gateway to the road (Park Lane) and alongside this is Cray High Bridge. It is possible to walk back to Buckden along the road. However, it is a much more pleasant journey returning along Buckden Rake and it is level or downhill walking all the way!

When you get back to Buckden you can get refreshments in the village restaurant and tea rooms or in the Buck Inn.

In the area:

Kilnsey Park (www.kilnseypark.co.uk; 01756 752150). This is a great countryside experience for the whole family all year round. Children can follow the fun trail around the park and hunt for clues, feed the ducks and play in the adventure playground. There is a fun pool where children of under 12 can experience fishing and take their catch home for tea! Visit the freshwater aquarium, farm shop and the restaurant and coffee shop. Open daily (9.00am-5.00pm during the summer).

Middleham Castle (www.middlehamonline.com; 01969 623899). The construction of the castle began around 1170 by Robert Fitzrandolph during the reign of Henry II. The castle has had many owners but in 1646, Parliament ordered much of it to be destroyed leaving the ruins that we see today. There is a shop selling snacks on site and plenty of room in the grounds for picnics. Open daily between March and September and everyday except Tuesday and Wednesday for the rest of the year.

Walk 15: The Nidderdale Way, Lofthouse

Allow: 2 hours

Nidderdale is the smallest of the principal dales but offers a huge variety of landscape and has been classified as an area of outstanding natural beauty. This walk takes you through some of this beautiful rolling countryside and part of the route uses a section of the Nidderdale Way. The Nidderdale Way is a 53-mile circular route which passes through the best scenery the area has to offer.

This is a fantastic walk for those who love the great outdoors. However, although the majority of the walk is on level ground there are a couple of tough sections. There is one uphill climb and a steep winding downhill that ends in a difficult dry river bed crossing. These obstacles are easy to negotiate with two people and make the walk a fun and absorbing experience.

Map: Ordnance Survey 1:25000 Explorer 298 – grid reference 099764

Distance: 3¾ miles

Getting there: Drive through Lofthouse in the direction of Middlesmoor. Straight after the bridge over the River Nidd turn right down the lane which is signposted to Scar House Reservoir. Drive down this road and park in the first parking area on the left after you have passed two picnic areas. There is a large bricked-up stone arch here which forms part of an old dismantled railway.

Turn left out of the car park and walk up the road with the River Nidd on your right.

1. After about fifteen minutes, turn right down a small lane to Summerstone Estate. Walk down the hill, cross the bridge over the river and turn immediately left following the riverside path.

Follow this dirt and stone track through the gateway and continue straight ahead.

When the path turns to the right away from the river, ignore the footpath that passes through a wall stile to your left, but go through the gateway ahead. Follow the grass track with the wall on your right to the next gateway.

Go through this gateway and the one ahead. Follow the track straight ahead with a barn on your left and a small stream on your right. The

Cow grazing in a Nidderdale pasture

track then curves round to the right following the stream uphill. This is the most strenuous section of the walk.

2. Follow the path as it bears left away from the stream until you come to a fork. Take the right-hand fork uphill and in just a few minutes you will see a footpath signpost ahead of you. At this junction turn right along the Nidderdale Way with the dry stone wall to your left.

Continue up the track and through a gateway. Cross a very small ford over the stream and follow the track ahead. This stony track takes you through a gateway and along to Newhouses Edge Farm. After passing the farm on your right the gravel track becomes flat and even. All the uphill walking is now over.

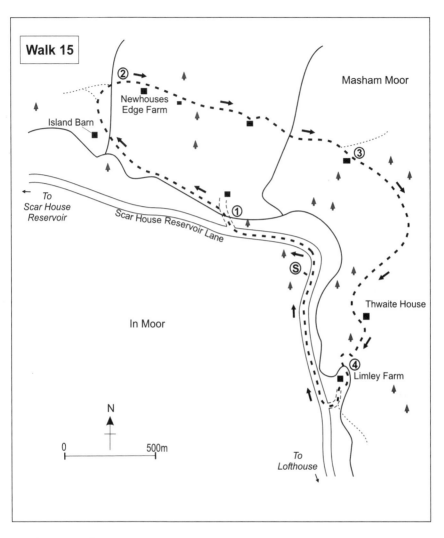

There are fantastic views across Nidderdale all along this track. In Moor and Woodale Scar can be seen on your right and Masham Moor to your left.

Keep following this track along, passing several houses on your right and going through any gateways you come across. After twenty five minutes you will pass a steep track up to your left. Ignore this and stay on the path ahead.

3. A couple of minutes later the track bends to the right and you will see a footpath signpost and a house ahead. Follow the track as it bends back to the left and through a gateway. The track then weaves its way down the hill with fantastic views all around.

After about ten minutes you will arrive at Thwaite House. Go through the gate and follow the path as it goes around the edge of the house and through the front garden. At the end of the garden turn right through the gateway following the footpath arrows.

The path is now a grassy track which goes steeply downhill; this can be overgrown with ferns in places. Be careful as all this downhill section is steep and can be very slippery. After a few minutes you will come to a junction where you turn left following the footpath arrows.

The path bends back to the right and steeply down towards a barn. There are some low stone steps to help you get your grip on the way down. When the barn is just in front of you the path then bends back to the left. This even grass path heads down towards Limley Farm.

4. You will see a gap in the stone wall on your right. Keep following the path straight ahead with the wall on your right. Go through the gateway ahead and you will almost immediately come to the dry river bed. It is possible to drag the pushchair backwards over the river but it is much easy to carry it! Once you have crossed this short stony section follow the track up to the farm.

Keep following the path up to the left and into the farmyard. Go up in between the buildings and turn left following the arrows. This takes you between two houses and along the lane away from the farm. Follow the lane round to the right and you will shortly come to the road that you drove in on.

Turn right onto the road and follow it along for fifteen minutes until you find the car park on your left. You will pass a picnic area on the way if you fancy stopping for a break before you drive away.

In the area:

How Stean Gorge (www.nidderdale.co.uk/howstean; 01423 755666). Narrow paths and footbridges take you down an 80ft ravine cut through limestone rock by How Stean Beck as it cascades its way down to the River Nidd. Take a trip into Tom Taylor's cave with a torch or let the little ones play in the children's play area. There is a restaurant on site serving meals, light bites and cakes. Open 10.00am-6.00pm from Easter to September but closed on Monday and Tuesday. Check the website for winter opening times.

The Forbidden Corner . A unique labyrinth of tunnels, chambers, follies and surprises contained within a four acre garden. See such delights as the Temple of the Underworld and a huge pyramid of translucent glass. This was voted as one of the best children's attractions in Yorkshire but is great for adults as well. Admission is by booking only (www.yorkshirenet.co.uk/theforbiddencorner; 01969 640638).

Walk 16: Druid's Temple, Ilton

Allow: *45 minutes*

Druid's Temple was an elaborate folly created as a second Stonehenge by William Danby (1752-1833) in order to relieve unemployment in the area. The folly consists of huge oval alters, menhirs, dolmens and other structures all hidden in the middle of forestry commission land. The trees open out in places to give great vistas of Leighton Reservoir in the valley below.

This is a fantastic place to explore, with something to see round every corner. The route takes you round the outside of the folly and finishes in the centre at the impressive temple. The walk is relatively short and so there is plenty of opportunity for a picnic.

Map: Ordnance Survey 1:25000 Explorer 298 – grid reference 177786

Distance: 1 mile

Getting there: Park in the Druid's Plantation car park at the end of Knowle Lane just north of Ilton.

To enter Druid's Plantation go through the anti-horse barrier alongside the gate in the car park. Turn immediately left and follow the broad grass track through the immature woodland.

There are great views over Ilton Moor to your left.

Continue following the path round, ignoring a turning down to a gateway on the left. A few minutes later you will see two separate stone dolmens on the right-hand side. Keep following the path straight ahead through the coniferous woodland.

Ten minutes later you see a path off to the left and ahead the path becomes rutted and boggy. Continue straight ahead but if you go through the trees to the right of the main path you can avoid the boggy section and then rejoin the path once you have passed it.

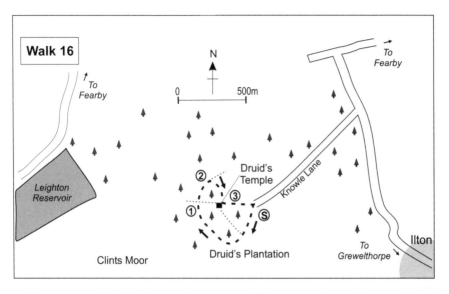

1. Just a couple of minutes later you will see another dolmen ahead of you in the centre of a crossroads. The walk continues on the path straight ahead.

If you have five minutes to spare it is worth taking the path to the left down to a gateway where there are great views of Leighton Reservoir and Clints Moor.

2. Follow the path round the edge of the woodland and you will pass a standing stone to your right. A few minutes later you will come to a junction. Take the turning to the right. Don't continue straight on as this is just a dead end.

The path heads back into the woodland. After five minutes you will come to a junction from which you will be able to see another standing stone to your right. Turn left away from the stone.

3. As you walk down this path the Druid's Temple will soon come into site.

It is worth spending some time looking round this amazing folly. There is a large stone seat, a sacrificial table in front of a grotto and much more. If you walk up the hill to the left of the temple you will see a tall stone stack and there is a great aerial view point over the temple.

Dolmen in Druid's Plantation

To continue the walk turn left (when you are facing the entrance to the temple). The path to the right takes you to the stone alter at the crossroads that you passed earlier. After five minutes this broad gravel track takes you back to the car park.

In the area:

Lightwater Valley (www.lightwatervalley.co.uk; 0870 4580040). A great family day out with a huge variety of rides for children of all ages. There is also a shopping village with a range of factory outlet shops and a Birds of Prey centre with over 60 birds and a creepy crawly reptile cave. The park is open from March to October between 10.00am–4.30pm.

Hackfall Woods (www.mashamshire.com/guide/hackfall). These woods can be found on the edge of Grewelthorpe. The land was brought by John Aislabie (see Walk 25: Studley Water Gardens) in 1731 and was turned into a beautiful wilderness complete with follies, grottoes and waterfalls by his son. The woods are now owned by the Woodland Trust and are a site of special scientific interest. Entrance is free.

Walk 17: Ingleborough Estate Nature Trail, Clapham

Allow: *2 hours*

This is a walk for all seasons that takes you through woodland to the open moorland below Thwaite scars. The paths are fantastic throughout and, although the outward route is all uphill, it is relatively easy pushing. The turning point for the walk is Ingleborough Cave. Tours can be taken in this show cave and refreshments are available at the cave shop.

The nature trail was created in 1970 to commemorate the local botanist, Reginald Farrer (1880-1920) and the European Conservation Year. Reginald Farrer collected many new species of rhododendrons and shrubs in China, Tibet and Upper Burma. Much of this plant collection can still be found within the Farrer families Ingleborough estate.

Map: Ordnance Survey 1:25000 Explorer OL2 – grid reference 745692

Distance: 3¼ miles

Getting there: Park in Clapham on Church Avenue either on the road side or in the pay and display car park. There are toilets in the car park.

Walk up the road towards the church, with the stream (Clapham Beck) on your left.

> There are several tea shops, a pub and various other shops within the village. There is also a children's play area and picnic tables on your left as you walk towards the church.

When you reach St James Church follow the road to the left and cross the bridge over the stream. Turn right up the road in the direction of Ingleborough Cave.

On your right you will be able to see Clapham Falls which flow from underneath a stone arch.

1. Follow the road around to the left and you will see a sign to Ingleborough Cave, Lake, Woods and Trail. Turn right up this path and follow it round to the right between the buildings until you see a barrier and a ticket machine. There is a small fee to pay to use the trail, and information leaflets (these describe numbered features along the route) can be found next to the

Enjoying an ice lolly at the end of Clapham Nature Trail

ticket machine. The outward journey follows a steady ascent but don't worry, you get to go down hill all the way back!

Follow the broad gravel track into the woodland. The path winds its way up the hill and takes you to a T-junction. Turn right and follow the path up the hill. You will soon see the lake on your right and there are several picnic benches along the route if you fancy a break.

Once you have passed the lake the path continues alongside Clapham Beck. Do not deviate from this path; stay on the route ahead which takes you all the way up to Ingleborough Cave.

The cliffs that you can see to your right are Thwaite Scars.

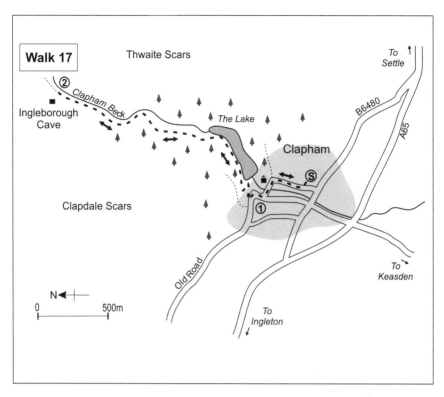

The path takes you through Clapdale Wood where you will see a large stone building to the left of the path called The Grotto.

The Grotto was built for shelter and its construction provided employment during the early 19th-century recession.

Go through the gateway at the end of the woodland and follow the track ahead with moorland to both sides.

2. After about an hour you will finally arrive at Ingleborough Show Cave where there is also a shop selling refreshments and ice creams.

Return by the same route.

In the area:

Ingleborough Cave (www.ingleboroughcave.co.uk; 015242 51242). The cave has attracted thousands of visitors since its discovery in 1837. Regular tours are conducted along the large and beautifully decorated passages. The cave can only be reached via the Ingleborough Estate Nature Trail. There is a shop at the entrance selling snacks and hot and cold drinks. Open 10.00am-5.00pm but winter tours are available by appointment only.

Settle to Carlisle Railway (www.settle-carlisle.co.uk; 08457 48 49 50). This is England's most scenic railway and even though it is part of the regular rail network and not a steam railway it is well worth taking a trip to check out the views. The whole route is 72 miles and takes you over Ribblehead Viaduct and through Blea Moor tunnel. This is a great way to see the Dales and a lovely alternative to the car.

Walk 18: Austwick to Wharfe

Allow: 2 hours 30 minutes

This is a great walk along easy green lanes and tracks. The walk begins at Austwick and also passes through the village of Wharfe. Austwick means 'settlement east of the main village' which was Clapham. The local economy used to be based on hand looming, weaving and farming. This is now a popular walking area as it has some of the best limestone scenery in the national park. Just above Austwick are the Norber erratics, large Silurian grit boulders which were carried here by a glacier over 12,000 years ago. Once the glacier melted the rocks were left on limestone pavement and since then rain water has dissolved the limestone around them leaving them on small stone pedestals.

The village has many tales associated with it and the best known of these is that of the Austwick cuckoo. It is said that the villagers noticed that the cuckoo arrived when the sun shone so they decided to capture one and with it the sunshine. They found a cuckoo roosting in a tree and proceeded to build a wall around it that night. The cuckoo flew off at sunrise before the last bricks where laid and since then Austwick has been known as Cuckoo Town.

Map: Ordnance Survey 1:25000 Explorer OL2 – grid reference 768686

Distance: 4¾ miles

Getting there: Drive through Austwick in the direction of Horton. After passing the Game Cock pub on your left, park on the roadside near the school.

Walk along the road away from the village centre and take the first turning on the left up the no-through road, Town Head Lane. Walk up this quiet country lane as it takes you gradually uphill and out of the village. As the hill levels out pass straight over a crossroads and continue up the lane (Crummack Lane).

There are great views
of Oxenber wood and
White Stone to your
right. The large crag to
your left is Robin
Proctor's Scar. Ahead
is a series of small
crags, Nappa Scars.

1. Continue along this
   lane as it turns from
   tarmac to gravel until
   you come to a junc-
   tion. Turn right along
   the bridleway sign-
   posted to Wharfe
   (White Stone Lane).
   The path ahead can be
   muddy.

The crags ahead are
Studrigg and White
Stone.

White Stone Lane

2. This track takes you to
   a ford over Austwick Beck. Cross the clapper bridge (Wash Dub
   Bridge) and continue along the track ahead. Just past the ford
   there is a gap in the wall to the right. There is a bench here and it
   makes a lovely picnic spot.

This is one of three clapper bridges within Austwick all of which are
made from blue-grey Horton flagstone. Next to the bridge is Wash
Dub field and in spring and autumn the Beck used to be dammed
here in order to make a pool in which sheep could be dipped to rid
them of skin parasites.

The track soon narrows to a small dirt and stone path between
two dry stone walls. The path is a little rockier now but easy to

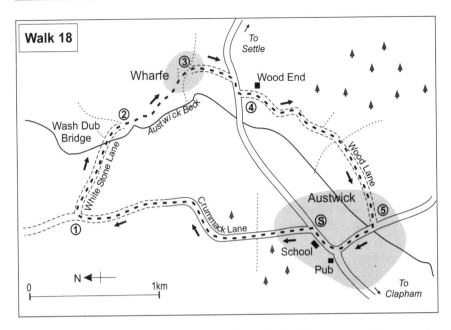

negotiate as it is heading gently down hill. The path widens again as you pass two barns and it heads down towards the village of Wharfe. At a fork in the path take the larger right-hand path which takes you down to some houses.

3. Turn left onto the broad gravel track through the centre of the village and then right at the next fork which takes you out of the village. Follow the lane all the way down to a road and turn right.

4. After a few minutes turn left up Wood End Farm Lane (signposted as a bridle way to Wood Lane). Turn right up a green lane just before you reach the farm. This track can be very muddy.

You will be able to see Austwick to your right and Oxenber Wood up to your left.

Follow this green lane as it bears left and then right again. Eventually you will come to a junction with a small track up to the wood on the left. Take the path to the right here and follow it as it narrows and takes you to a crossroads. Go straight ahead onto a broad green lane (Wood Lane).

The track to your right is an alternative route back to the car which takes you over Flascoe Bridge, another clapper footbridge.

5. Follow the track all the way back to the road. Turn right and cross over Austwick Bridge. Follow the road back up into the village. At the next junction (grass triangle) turn right in the direction of Horton and pass the post office on your right.

Walk up the road past the Game Cock pub and find your car by the school.

In the area:

The Watershed Mill and Visitor Centre, Settle. This cotton mill has been converted into a visitor's centre and has a range of shops including a Yorkshire Ale shop, Country Kitchen, Edinburgh Woollen Mill, and a coffee shop. Open seven days a week 10.00am-5.30pm (www.watershedmill.co.uk; 01729 825539).

Settle Swimming Pool. This 20m heated pool is a great way to entertain the kids when the weather is bad. There are water baby and family sessions. Also have fun with inflatable toys in the pool during the summer holidays. Phone ahead for opening times (www.settle.org.uk/settle+swimming+pool; 01729 823626).

Walk 19: Malham Tarn

Allow: *2 hrs*

Malham Tarn was declared a wetland of international importance by the Ramfar convention and is home to a unique community of plants and animals. The alkaline waters are fed by streams off the limestone hills and the shallow lake supports primitive plants and a rare white clawed crayfish. This is the only site in the UK for a rare endangered wingless caddis fly and many wildfowl including Great Crested Grebe nest here. Alongside the lake is Tarn Moss, an important area of raised bog and fen. The bog supports Sphagnum moss and heather and many rare plants including Northern March Orchids.

This is a nice relaxing walk through woodland and open moor and it has the added bonus that you can shorten it to suit. If you decide that you have already walked far enough simply turn around and retrace your footsteps. Malham Tarn is on a high area of Malham Moor and can be quite exposed so if the weather is windy don't forget to wrap up warm.

Map: Ordnance Survey 1:25000 Explorer OL2 – grid reference 882671

Distance: 4 miles

Getting there: Park in the small quarry parking area on Cove Road near the Malham Tarn Nature Reserve and Field Centre.

Turn right and walk down the road for a short distance. Turn left through a gateway onto a broad track between two stone walls.

> On your right is Tarn Moss which is part of Malham Tarn Nature Reserve, an internationally important wetland area. Access is by permit only.

1. After 15 minutes you will reach a T-junction. Turn right onto the private road. Go through the gate to the right of the cattle grid and follow the road all the way to Malham Tarn Field Studies Centre.

Path alongside Malham Tarn

You will pass through an area of woodland and will catch glimpses of the tarn on your right. There is a stone boat house on the edge of the tarn and then a viewing platform with an information board.

2. When you arrive at the field centre turn left, following the Pennine Way footpath sign. The track circles round the back of the building and bears left just before a parking area.

The track passes through more woodland and eventually brings you to another cattle grid. Go through the gateway up to the left of this grid and then rejoin the broad gravel track as it passes alongside the tarn.

There are fantastic views over the tarn to your right and on your left is Great Close Hill, a large rocky outcrop.

Go through another gateway and immediately after this take the footpath to the right signposted as the Pennine Way, Water Sinks Gate. This takes you off the gravel track and onto a grassy moorland path.

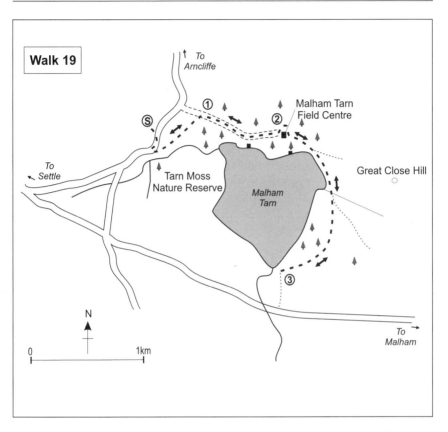

You will come to a faint fork in the track, take the path to the right which follows the dry stone wall. At the next corner of the wall go straight ahead and walk towards the tarn. This path leads you up to Tarn Foot where a stream flows away from the tarn.

On a hot day this is a lovely place for a picnic, with great views over the tarn.

3. This is the turning point for the walk so simply return to the car park by the same route.

There is a second car park just past Tarn Foot. If you are walking with a group of people it would be possible to leave one car here and then the walk can be done in one direction only.

In the area:

Yorkshire Dales Trekking Centre, Malham (www.ydtc.net; 01729 830352). This is an activity for those with older kids. The trekking centre breeds its own Dales ponies which it uses to take riders aged 8 and older on short or long treks over a variety of terrain.

Pennine Boat Trips of Skipton (www.canaltrips.co.uk; 01756 790829). Take a cruise on a barge down the 200-year-old Leeds to Liverpool Canal. Cruises run most days between Easter and October. Return trips are 1 hour 15 minutes and refreshments and toilets are available on board.

Walk 20: Malham Cove

Allow: *1 hour 45 minutes*

Once a massive waterfall would have poured over the top of Malham Cove from a large glacier melting on the high land above. A stream now emerges at the base of the cove but freezing water and rain have continued to shape the huge (250ft) limestone cliff face that we see today. Investigations of the cave behind the cove suggest that it was formed 50,000 years ago, much earlier than previously thought. On the top of the cove is a wide expanse of remarkable limestone pavement where the water has worked its way down through the weaker sections of this soluble rock.

The walk starts in Malham where there are a variety of shops, tea shops and pubs. The route then takes you along green lanes and up to the base of the cove. It is possible to reach the limestone pavement on top but you will have to leave the pushchair behind. The outward tracks on this circular walk can be bumpy and stony in places. If you want to avoid this simply do a there and back walk approaching the cove via the road (markers 3 & 4 on map).

Map: Ordnance Survey 1:25000 Explorer OL2 – grid reference 900627

Distance: 3 miles

Getting there: Park in the National Park car park, Malham. There are toilets with baby changing facilities and a picnic area next to the National Park visitor's centre.

Walk out of the car park along the entrance road. Turn right up a stone track marked as a footpath before you reach the main road. Turn right at the first junction towards Pikedaw.

> As you walk up the track, Malham village is on the right and you should soon be able to see Malham Cove ahead.

Malham Cove

1. When you reach a junction in the path turn left up the stony track. There is a footpath arrow on the gatepost to your left. Follow this track uphill until you pass the Malham Water Treatment building on the left. Turn right as the track forks onto the grass and stone path.

   There are fantastic views of the Cove and the limestone pavement above it to your right and great views across the dales all around you.

2. Go through the gateway and follow the path across the grassy meadow to another gateway onto Cove Road. Turn right and walk down the road towards the Cove.

3. Turn left onto the Pennine Way footpath to the cove. This immediately takes you through two small gates and along a flat gravel path. Follow this path along and pass through a gate to the left of a kissing gate. The path then runs alongside Malham Beck.

4. Go through another gate and when the path forks turn right. This

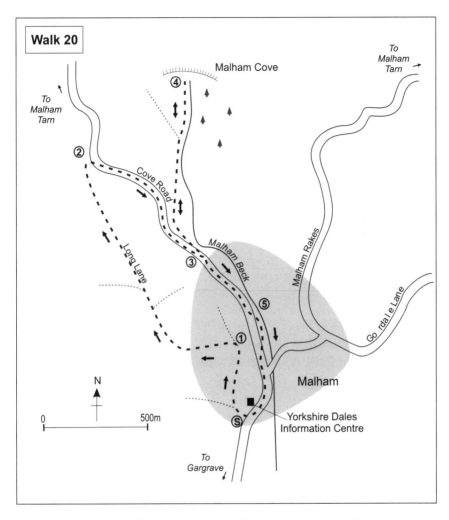

takes you to the foot of the cove. There are plenty of grassy areas to stop for a picnic alongside the Beck.

The left fork takes you up a long series of steps to the limestone pavement on top of the cove. This is definitely not pushchair friendly but well worth the effort for any 'baby free' walkers in the group.

Return along the same track to the road. Turn left and walk down the hill towards Malham village. Pass a turning to the left towards Beck Hall B&B, where you will see an old clapper bridge.

5. Immediately after the clapper bridge turn left through a small gateway on to a woodland path that runs alongside the beck.

Follow this path until you come to another gateway back onto the road and then follow the road left down into the village and all the way back to the car park.

There are several pubs and tea shops in the village as well as several shops.

In the area:

Kirkby Field Farm Centre, Malham gives kids a great opportunity to touch and feed a variety of animals. There are both traditional and rare farm animals as well as some more exotic animals. There are sheepdog handling demonstrations, a children's play area and a picnic area where you can get light snacks. Opening times are seasonal so ring before you go.
(www.malhamdale.com/kirkbyfield.htm; 01729 830487)

Malham Safari Trail (www.malhamdale.com). This is a great day out for all the family but only happens for a few days around the end of May or the beginning of June each year (ask at the National Park Centre or check out the dates on line). Take a gentle stroll round the village to find the animals and complete the quiz. There is also a duck race, a balloon race, face painting and a bouncy castle.

Walk 21: Grass Wood Nature Reserve, Grassington

Allow: *1 hour 30 minutes or 2 hours*

Grass Wood is an ancient ash woodland over limestone scars owned by Yorkshire Wildlife Trust. This nature reserve has a rich ground flora and also a number of bird species including woodpeckers. The wood is gradually being regenerated through conifer removal and replanting of broadleaf trees. Grass Wood is the largest individual remnant of native broadleaf woodland in the whole of the Yorkshire Dales.

This is a lovely tranquil walk which gives you plenty of opportunity to absorb the beauty of your surroundings. The route takes you past a Brigantine fort, Fort Gregory, which was built against Roman invasion. There is also the option of extending the walk to the site of a medieval village (which was wiped out by the Black Death) in the south-east corner of the wood.

Map: Ordnance Survey 1:25000 Explorer OL2 – grid reference 984651

Distance: 2½ or 3¼ miles

Getting there: Drive along Grass Wood Lane from Grassington to Conistone. Park in the small car park on the right in Grass Wood.

Walk out of the car park back onto the road and turn left. In a couple of minutes turn left to a gateway into Grass Wood. Lift the pushchair over the low stile and follow the path as it bears up to the left. At the next junction turn left so that you are walking along with the wooden fence on your right.

1. Follow this narrow woodland path all the way to a clearing. There is a notice board here telling you all about the wood. Turn right and follow the broad track as it begins to head uphill. Follow the path as it bends to the right in the direction of Grassington.

Grass Wood

Continue to follow the path uphill passing straight over a small crossroads.

2. The path then begins to level out and you will shortly see a faint grass path off to the right. To do the shorter version of the walk turn right here. Then follow directions from ****

If you want to do the extra loop to the site of the Medieval Settlement then continue straight ahead on the main path. Go straight over a signposted crossroads in the direction of Grassington. Follow the path as it heads gently downhill with a limestone scar to the left.

3. You will see a path joining the main track from the right. This is the return route. However, to continue to the Iron Age Settlement follow the path ahead for a few more minutes and you will come to a clearing with a sign for the 'prehistoric settlement of national importance', the Iron Age Fort is here.

To continue the walk return back along the path for a few minutes

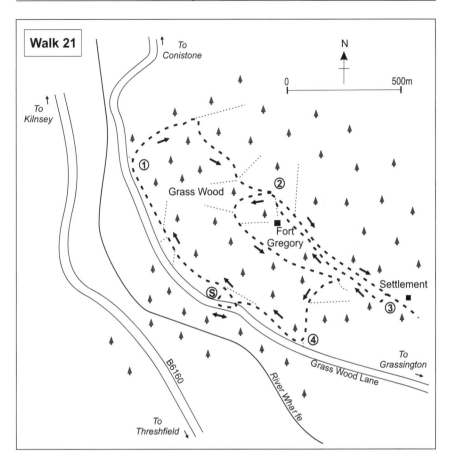

until you come to a fork. Turn left here onto a small woodland path. Follow this undulating path as it climbs along the top of Gregory Scar.

There are some great views across Wharfedale from this path.

Continue to follow this path until it eventually returns you to the broad track you were on earlier (marker 2 on map). Turn left on to this track and then turn almost immediately left again along a faint grass path that heads back into the woodland.

****The path goes uphill for a short distance and then there is a steady descent back to the bottom of the wood. Pass straight over a small crossroads (there is a path to Fort Gregory on the left here). Continue to follow the path straight ahead as a second path joins from the right. Follow the path as it bends round to the right and then go left at the next junction. Turn right at the following junction.

4. Follow this path as it goes down towards a gateway onto Grass Wood Lane. Turn right just before you get to this gateway and follow the path along with a dry stone wall down to your left.

   Go left at the fork in the track and follow it back down to the gateway at which you entered the wood. Lift the pushchair over the stile, turn right onto the road and in a few minutes you will see the car park on the right.

In the area:

Upper Wharfedale Museum, Grassington (01756 752800). The museum is open daily between April and October 2.00-4.30pm and has displays on farming and industry in the Dales over the years. There is also an exhibit of veterinary equipment and a mineral collection.

Craven Swimming Pool, Skipton . If the weather is bad why not take the kids for a swim? This centre has both a large 25m pool and a small training pool suitable for babies and toddlers. There is also a café for refreshments after your swim.
(www.cravendc.gov.uk/craven/visitors/leisure/
cravenswimmingpool; 01756 792805)

Walk 22: Grassington Moor Lead Mine Trail

Allow: *1 hour 30 minutes*

Grassington has a long history of lead mining that dates back to the 15th century when monks from Fountains Abbey worked a smelt mill. The industry really took off in the 18th and 19th centuries when large numbers of people were employed in the mines and smelt mills at Grassington Moor and Yarnbury. The mineral rights were owned by the Duke of Devonshire and he built a large smelt mill and provided the drainage systems for the deep mines. The industry went into decline with the advent of the Cotton Mills and had finished by the early 20th century. Tourism has been the main industry since that time.

This fascinating route takes you along part of the mine trail, past what remains of Beever Reservoir, Cupola Smelt Mill, High Windings Dam and the chimney. The paths are excellent throughout with any stony area easily avoided. Be aware that this walk is across a high moorland area and consequently can be quite exposed so make sure you wrap up well.

Map: Ordnance Survey 1:25000 Explorer OL2 – grid reference 015658

Distance: 2¾ miles

Getting there: Drive up the no-through road (Moor Lane) from Grassington village centre to Yarnbury. Park on the grass verge at the end of the surfaced road.

Leave the parking area and go through the gateway on the left at the end of the surfaced road. This is signposted as a bridleway to Hebden and there is an information board about the mine trail here.

1. Follow this broad gravel path until you come to a fork. Turn left and follow the path through two gateways (both with ladder stiles

Grassington Moor Lead Mine Trail

alongside) all the way up to the mine buildings. (These gateways are usually unlocked even when there appears to be a padlock there!).

There are many places to stop and explore on route and most of the mine relics have information boards describing there function.

2. Stay on this track and it takes you up between High Grinding Mill and a large chimney.

There is a path to the chimney if you want to take a closer look.

3. Not long after you have passed the mill you will come to a cross-roads. Turn left and follow the path as it bears back round to the left. Go through the gateway next to a wooden enclosure and follow the track all the way back to your car. There are some stony sections here but the worst can usually be avoided.

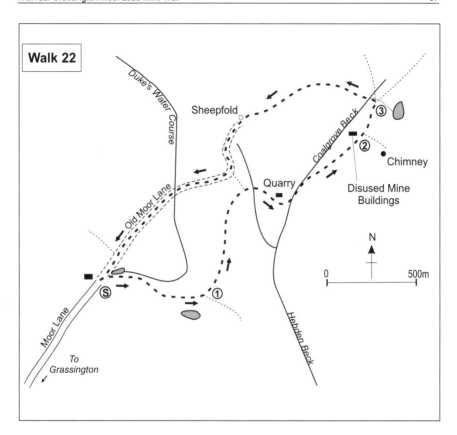

In the area:

Parcevall Hall Gardens (www.parcevallhallgardens.co.uk; 01756 720311). 16 acres of formal and woodland gardens with great views of Simon's Seat and Wharfedale. The gardens were designed by William Milner and planted with specimen trees and shrubs from Western China and the Himalayas. There are tea rooms on site, a picnic area and a shop.

Kilnsey Trekking and Riding Centre (www.kilnseyriding.com; 01756 752861). Pony treks of varied length are available for anyone over the age of 4. Under 7's must be accompanied by an adult on foot. Riding lessons also provided at the centre.

Walk 23: Pateley Bridge Panorama and River Trail

Allow: *1 hour 45 minutes*

Pateley Bridge is a picturesque town in the heart of Nidderdale. The town has an industrial past with many breweries, quarries and flax mills operating in the 1700s. Agriculture is now the main industry and the annual Nidderdale Show is held here. The narrow high street has plenty of shops, tea rooms and cafés to visit including the oldest sweet shop in England.

This is a great route which follows the panorama walk from Pateley Bridge giving spectacular views over Nidderdale and the moors beyond. The route passes through the model village of Glasshouses, which was established for mill and quarry workers in the 1800s, and returns via a picturesque path alongside the River Nidd. The walk has been given a hard grading because of the steep section at the beginning. However, all the paths are good and even.

Map: Ordnance Survey 1:25000 Explorer 298 – grid reference 157655

Distance: 3½ miles

Getting there: Park in any of the Pateley Bridge car parks next to the bridge over the River Nidd.

Make your way to the bottom of High Street, the main road through the centre of town, and walk up the road into town with the bridge behind you.

> There are plenty of tea shops and pubs in Pateley Bridge. Half way up the high street there is a great sweet shop which also sells ice cream. This shop is reputed to be the oldest sweet shop (1827) in England.

1. At the top of High Street follow the road around to the right onto

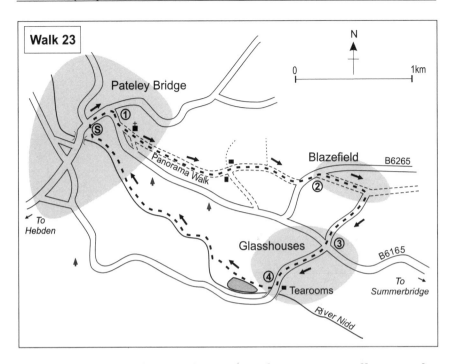

Ripon Road. Cross over the road so that you are walking on the left-hand side. After a few minutes, just after the Methodist church, go up the steps on your left signposted to Panorama walk. There are just a few steps here and they are the only steps on the route.

This first section of the walk is steep but there are a couple of benches on route if you fancy a rest. There are fantastic panoramic views over Nidderdale to the right on the whole of this first section of the walk.

Stay on this path until you reach Pateley Bridge Cemetery. Pass the cemetery and continue up the hill, don't take the turning to the left here.

Look out for a small gate on the right which takes you to a great view point.

When you reach a junction in the path follow the route straight

The view over Nidderdale from Panorama Walk

ahead to Blazefield. Shortly after this you come to a fork in the path, take the left-hand path along the Nidderdale Way. This is now a gravel and grass track. Stay on this track ignoring the public footpath you will pass on your left. This section of the track gets narrow and overgrown in places.

At the next fork in the track take the right-hand path down the hill. The path is now a dirt track with small stones which finally brings you to a road (Blazefield Bank). Turn left and walk up this quiet country lane being careful of any cars.

2. Just before the first house on the right (as you enter the village of Blazefield) there is a small lane, signposted as 'Nidderdale Way' and 'Access Only Bridlepath'. This track passes in front of a row of houses.

   You will be able to see woodland in the distance ahead of you. Behind this is Brimham Moor and Brimham Rocks. To the right you will be able to see the rocky outcrop Guise Cliff.

As you pass the houses Rock Haven and Rock House the track

bears down to the right. This takes you to another country lane, Sandy Lane, where you turn right and follow the road downhill.

3. Go straight over the crossroads across the main road (B6165) and into Glasshouses. To the left of the turning to Glasshouses there are some public toilets. You will soon pass the village shop which sells ice cream! Continue walking down through the village passing the village green on your right. This brings you down to the bridge over the River Nidd.

On your left before the bridge is Yorkshire Country Wines Tearooms, which sells hot and cold food and has high chairs.

4. Just before the bridge is a track on the right signposted as a public footpath. Walk along this broad gravel track which takes you past a lake on the left. Stay on this main path ignoring other tracks off to the left.

After 10 minutes the path adjoins the river at a weir. Stay on this lovely riverside track which takes you all the way back to Pateley Bridge. You will pass Harefield Hall Hotel, a car park and picnic area, and some benches on the left. Finally you will see the High Street to your right where the walk began.

In the area:

There is a children's playground in Pateley Bridge park and an ice cream van is often parked here too.

Nidderdale Museum (www.nidderdalemuseum.com; 01423 711225). Step back in time and see how people used to live in the Dales. There are eleven rooms of exhibits including a cobbler's shop, school room and Victorian parlour. Open 1.30-4.30pm from Easter to November.

Stump Cross Caverns (www.stumpcrosscaverns.co.uk; 01756 752780). This show cave is open daily from 10.00am between mid-March and the end of October. There are a large range of stalactites and stalagmites, and unusual rock formations on show as you walk along the pathways down into the caves. There is a tea room for refreshments after your trip.

Walk 24: Brimham Rocks, Summerbridge

Allow: 1 hour

This is a great little walk around some of the strangest rock formations in Yorkshire. Although the majority of paths are good the nature of this site means that there are some rocks to negotiate, therefore it is worth having two people on the walk.

Brimham rocks appear in the Domesday Book and four centuries of monks from Fountains Abbey developed and farmed this land. The rocks are stacks of millstone grit formed by erosion since glacial times. This has left many interesting rock formations which have been a popular tourist destination for the last 200 years. The strange shapes have been given many different names from Druids writing desk to Dancing Bear. The moorland surrounding the rocks is mainly heather and bilberry and birds such as curlew, snipe, grouse and mallard can be seen as well as sheep, red deer and hares.

A leaflet detailing the area and the main formations can be purchased at the National Trust shop. There is also a snack kiosk and toilets with baby changing facilities on site.

Map: Ordnance Survey 1:25000 Explorer 298 – grid reference 208645

Distance: 1½ miles

Getting there: Park in the National Trust car park at Brimham Rocks.

Follow the main path from the car park up towards the rocks. You will go past a wooden gate and a notice board with a map of the area. After a few minutes take the smaller left-hand path which goes towards the shop and toilets. Stay on this path ignoring any tracks off to the sides.

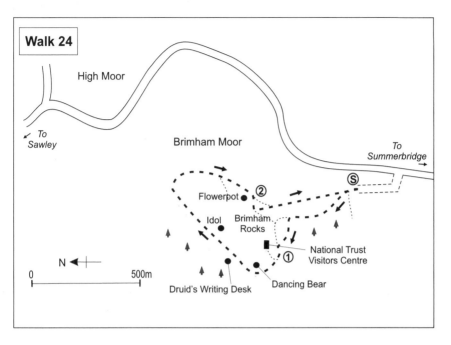

There are plenty of grassy areas around the whole site where you ′ can stop for a picnic.

1. At the end of the path you will see a café and shop in front of you. Turn left and follow the track round. Where the main track turns right towards the shop go up the smaller gravel track to the left.

   Soon you will see the Dancing Bear formation on your right. Shortly after this there is a clearing on your left and you will be able to see the Druid's writing desk.

   Follow the path round and after a few minutes you will pass the idol formation on your right. Soon there will be a clearing to the left with great views over High Moor. Follow the path round to the right, not straight ahead to the moorland. The path then becomes much more even.

2. Pass the next formation, the flowerpot, and then join the path going left so the formation is behind you. At the next clearing turn right onto a wider grassy path which allows you to miss an

awkward section. Turn left at the top of this path and then almost immediately the path forks. Take the left-hand fork which heads downwards and then turn right to join another path.

Eventually the path leads you down to the car park where, if you are lucky, you will find an ice cream van!

In the area:

Nidderdale Pool and Leisure Centre, Pateley Bridge. If it's raining why not take the kids to this 20m swimming pool?

The Idol, Brimham Rocks

There is also a gym, squash and badminton courts and play schemes in the holidays. (www.harrogate.gov.uk/sportandleisure; 01423 711442)

Yorkshire Country Wines. Take a guided tour of the winery and taste the traditional fruit wines produced here. Visit the idyllic riverside tearooms housed in a 19th-century flax mill (www.yorkshirecountrywines.co.uk; 01423 711947).

Walk 25: Studley Water Gardens, Ripon

Allow: 2 hours

Studley Water Gardens and Deer Park were created by John Aislabie MP and his son William from 1716 onwards and are one of the few remaining green gardens to remain in there original form. They canalised the River Skell and made vistas between the two important local landmarks, Ripon Cathedral and Fountains Abbey. The valley of the seven bridges was created where the criss-cross path of the river was made accessible via fords and stone bridges for both pedestrians and carriages. Geometric ponds, cascades, temples and towers were constructed to complete the spectacular water garden.

This walk takes you through the deer park and along the seven bridges walk. There are fantastic views throughout and ample spots for picnicking. The terrain is good throughout and, if the weather is hot, you can cool your feet down in one of the many fords!

Map: Ordnance Survey 1:25000 Explorer 298 – grid reference 272686

Distance: 4 miles

Getting there: Park in the National Trust Studley Water Gardens car park just off Church Walk. Make your way to the visitor's centre where there is a gift shop, restaurant, ice cream parlour and toilets with baby changing facilities.

When you leave the visitor's centre walk straight ahead following signs for St Mary's Church, Deer Park and Water Garden. This brings you immediately to a wooden gate. Go through this, cross the road and follow the path to the left.

1. After 10 minutes you will come to a crossroads where you go straight ahead. A few minutes later you will see a gate on your right with a sign 'Private Road Estate Vehicles Only'. Go through

St Mary's Church, Studley Deer Park

the small gate to the right of this which takes you onto the road
through the estate with St Mary's Church on your left.

St Mary's Church was built between 1871-8 for the Marquess and
Marchioness of Ripon by William Burges. As well as being a focal
point on the Studley Royal Estate the interior of the church is
beautiful. Ripon Cathedral can be seen when looking down the lime
tree avenue through the Deer Park from the church. As you are now
in the Deer Park keep a lookout for these impressive animals. There
are three species of deer in this 400-acre park, Red, Fallow and
Manchurian Sika, all of which are protected species.

Follow this tarmac lane passing the church and then the Choris-
ters House on your left. After about 10 minutes take the second
turning on the right which goes downhill towards the lake. Just
before you reach the lake turn left onto a small stony path and
follow this round with the lake on your right.

The lake is entirely man-made and used to have a carriage road
right round the perimeter. On the other side of the lake there is a
museum, shop and refreshments.

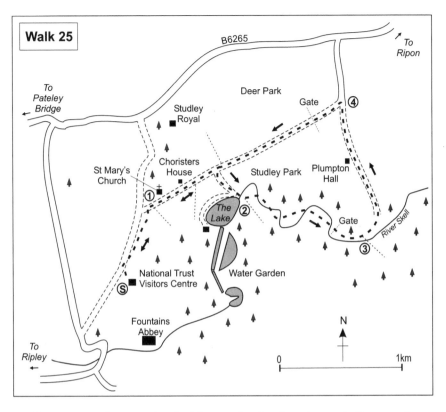

2. Cross over the wooden bridge or the ford and turn left away from the lake. Then take the left-hand fork which follows the route of the River Skell. After a few minutes turn left across the grass and cross the stone bridge ahead. Turn right following the riverside path immediately after the bridge.

You are now on the seven bridges walk. Follow the path and cross the next three stone bridges or, if the river is low enough, go through the fords. Make sure you stick to the path that follows the river; don't take any tracks off this path.

Cross the fifth stone bridge and you will see a tall kissing gate immediately ahead of you. This kissing gate is a very tight squeeze but with a bit of shuffling it is possible to get the push-chair through. However, you may find it quicker and easier to remove the little one from the buggy and fold it down.

You are now in the Chinese Wood. On the other side of the river is Mackershaw Wood.

3. Follow the path along, passing a small green footbridge on your right. Do not cross this bridge. You will leave the seven bridges walk at this point and follow the bridleway around the outside of the estate.

The path opens out with fields on both sides with great views over Ripon on your right. Follow this track as it passes Plumpton Hall on the left. Ten minutes later you will see a cottage on your right. Turn left here, next to the cattle grid, and you will see a large stone archway in front of you and St Mary's Church in the distance. This is the East Entrance to the Studley Royal Estate.

4. Follow this road all the way through the Deer Park and back to St Mary's Church. Go through the gate at the end of the road (this is where you entered the park originally) and turn left onto the path that runs alongside the road. At the end of this track turn left along the route signposted to the visitor's centre and car park. Cross the road and go through the wooden gate to the visitor's centre.

In the area:

Fountains Abbey (www.fountainsabbey.org.uk; 01765 608888). Walk around the ruins of this Cistercian Abbey founded in 1132 by monks from York. Extend your walk into the grounds of Studley Water Gardens and visit the numerous museums and tea shops on site. Baby feeding and changing facilities on site. Open daily 10.00am-4.00pm.

Big Sheep and Little Cow, Bedale (www.farmattraction.co.uk; 01677 422125). Bottle feed lambs and calves, bath Bruce the pig, hold and stroke the animals and take a pony ride. Quad bikes are available for kids between 6-12yrs. Go on a guided tour, visit the coffee shop and then try the farm-made ice cream. Open daily 10.30am-5.00pm from Easter to the end of October and Wednesday to Sunday the rest of the year.

Walk 26: Leeds and Liverpool Canal, East Marton

Allow: *1 hour 45 minutes*

The Leeds and Liverpool Canal was built in 1790 to provide a link between the ports of Liverpool and Hull. The canal was to provide a vital transport mechanism for the Yorkshire wool trade which had been developing steadily in the preceding years. However, the canals fell into disuse with the advent of the railways and in 1876 the Leeds to Carlisle railway was in operation. The canal has not carried any commercial traffic since 1954 but is in frequent use by the tourist industry.

This is the only canal walk in the book and it is definitely worth a look. The walk begins at Williamson Bridge and takes an easy saunter out to Newton Grange on quiet green lanes. The return route is along the canal towpath which winds its way back to the bridge through beautiful tranquil countryside. If you go in late summer you may be lucky enough to find wild raspberries which grow in abundance along the towpath, a rare treat these days.

Map: Ordnance Survey 1:25000 Explorer OL2 – grid reference 911511

Distance: 3½ miles

Getting there: When travelling on the A59 from Skipton to Clitheroe take the turning on the right towards Bank Newton next to The Cross Keys pub. Drive down this road, passing the riding stables and park in the lay by on the right immediately after the first canal bridge (Williamson Bridge).

1. Walk down the road away from the stables and canal bridge. After about five minutes you will come to a fork in the road. Take the right-hand road down towards Bank Newton. After a further twenty minutes you will come to Newton Grange Farm. Continue on the track between the farm and surrounding houses.

Leeds and Liverpool Canal, East Marton

2. Ten minutes later turn left through a wooden gate onto the canal path. Stay on the path for about an hour, passing through several wooden gates on your way.

You will see Newton Grange Farm down on you left and fantastic views over the Yorkshire Dales.

3. Pass under the first canal bridge and then five minutes later you will come to a second bridge marked 162. This is Williamson Bridge where the walk began. Go under the bridge and take the path up to the left and you will see your car in the lay by on the right.

In the area:

Skipton Castle (www.skiptoncastle.co.uk; 01756 792442). This 900-year-old castle is one of the best preserved medieval castles in England. Every corner of the castle is open to be explored, from banqueting halls to dungeons. There is also a picnic area, tea room and shop. The castle is open daily from 10.00am-6.00pm.

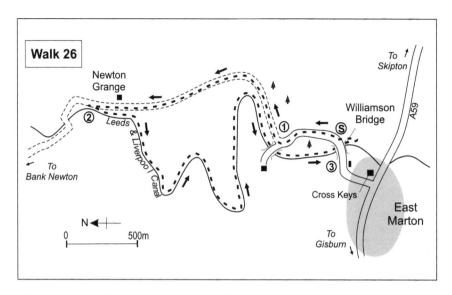

Skipton Woods (www.woodland-trust.org.uk). These woods are located next to the castle and once provided for all the castle's needs. There are at least 17 tree species here and plenty of wildlife including bats and deer. The woods are managed by the Woodland Trust and are a great place to escape and soak up some fantastic views. Spend a couple of hours and follow the Eller Beck valley on the 'Wild about Woods' trail. Free admission and open all year.

Walk 27: Bolton Abbey and The Strid

Allow: *1 hour 45 minutes (The Strid)/1 hour (Bolton Abbey)*

There are many possible walks on this large estate owned by the Duke of Devonshire. I have chosen two routes which can be undertaken as two separate short walks or one long one. Whatever you chose the well-maintained paths make these walks relatively easy going and suitable for all seasons.

Bolton Priory is an impressive site on the banks of the River Wharfe. It was built between the 12th and 14th centuries by Augustinian monks who prospered through their extensive lead mining and wool interests. The priory was destroyed by Henry VIII in 1540 as part of the dissolution of the monasteries. A church still exists on the site alongside the old priory ruins.

Strid Wood lies to the north of Bolton Priory and within the wood lies a deep and narrow section of the River Wharfe known as The Strid. Billions of gallons of water over hundreds of thousands of years have eroded the rocky bed of the river. This gorge is 30ft deep and rapid water with strong under currents flows through it. Strid actually means stride and many foolish people have tried to jump the gap which has claimed many lives. Legend has it that a white horse appears when someone is about to drown here.

Map: Ordnance Survey 1:25000 Explorer OL2 – grid reference 078551

Distance: The Strid – 2¾ miles/Bolton Abbey – 2 miles

Getting there: Park in Cavendish Pavilion car park on the Bolton Abbey Estate. There are picnic tables, tea rooms, a shop and toilets with baby changing facilities here.

Walk A – Bolton Priory

1. Walk towards Cavendish Pavilion and turn right crossing over the bridge towards the Valley of Desolation. Turn right down the footpath immediately after the bridge onto the riverside path towards Bolton Priory.

2. Go through the wooden gate and follow the track to the left. Turn right onto the tarmac lane and cross the ford (this can be avoided if you follow the path ahead, over a bridge and back to the road).

Take the next footpath on the right which goes to Bolton Priory. Follow this dirt and gravel path as it winds its way through the woodland. At the fork in the track turn left, pass through a gate

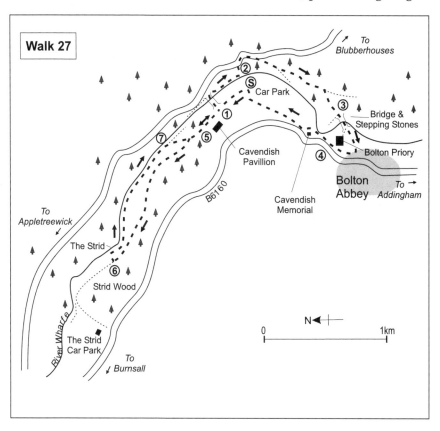

and then follow the path as it heads downhill to the river, ignoring a further turning up to the left.

There are fantastic views of the priory from this side of the river.

3. Turn left when you reach the river, go down a few steps and cross the footbridge. Go through the gate and follow the path straight ahead. Pass through the kissing gate and turn immediately right. Go through a metal gate and turn right towards the priory.

There are several benches next to the priory and an information board which tells you of the priory history.

4. The path goes past the priory entrance and takes you to a kissing gate next to the road. Turn right and walk along the footpath which runs alongside the road. This takes you to Cavendish monument. The footpath is now unsuitable for pushchairs so follow the road down to the car park going through two kissing gates on the way.

Walk B – The Strid

Walk past Cavendish Pavilion on your left keeping the River Wharfe on your right.

5. When you reach the wooden railings enter into the woodland (Strid Wood) and continue on the path straight ahead. This is signposted as Strid Nature Trails.

After five minutes take the left-hand fork up between two wooden bollards. The path goes uphill through the woodland and then levels out. Stay on the path as it turns to the right following the blue arrow.

6. You will eventually come to a junction in the path and you should be able to see a lookout shelter ahead. Turn right down the hill and the track leads you to a riverside path. There is an information board here and The Strid is the narrow section of river to your left.

The Strid is the narrow rocky area of the river. Be careful as the river is very dangerous here. There is a picnic table and several benches.

Once you have had a look at the Strid head back along the riverside path. Pass the notice board telling you about the wildlife, do not turn right here but keep straight ahead.

This is a lovely walk on picturesque river banks; there are several benches if you want to stop and admire the view. The broad, even path makes this an easy walk back.

The Strid, Bolton Abbey

7. When you come to a fork in the path, turn right, not left to Lud Stream Islands.

After five minutes you will come to another junction; continue straight ahead, not left down the steps or right up the path you walked out on.

Stay on this main path until you see a wooden fence and some notice boards ahead. Go through the gap in the fence and you are now back at Cavendish Pavilion. Find your car in the car park.

In the area:

Embsay & Bolton Abbey Steam Railway. Take a trip on a steam train through the beautiful Wharfedale countryside. Trains run every Sunday throughout the year and up to seven days a week during the summer. There is a café and shop at both Bolton Abbey and Embsay stations (www.embsayboltonabbeyrailway.org.uk; 01756 710614).

Hesketh Farm Park (www.heskethfarmpark.com; 01756 710444). Visit a modern working farm and meet the animals that live there. Wander through the straw maze, take a pony ride, go on the tractor and trailer tour or play in the outdoor playground. Opening days vary depending on time of year so check online before you go.

Walk 28: Swinsty Reservoir, Blubberhouses

Allow: *1 hour 45 minutes*

This is a great level pushchair walk along forestry paths and well-made tracks. The route goes around the reservoir and gives wonderful views across the water and surrounding countryside.

Swinsty reservoir is one of a chain of reservoirs in the Washburn Valley which supply water to Leeds. The reservoir was built in 1876 and holds approximately four million cubic meters of water. The reservoir is popular with fisherman as it is stocked with rainbow trout and there is a fishing office and training centre in the reservoir car park. Some of the land surrounding the reservoir has been set aside as a nature reserve so look out for a variety of water birds while you are on your walk.

Map: Ordnance Survey 1:25000 Explorer 297 – grid reference 186537

Distance: 3¼ miles

Getting there: Park in Swinsty Moor Fishing Office car park on North Lane. There are picnic tables and toilets here.

Go to the left-hand corner of the car park (close to the fishing office) and take the left-hand footpath, not the public bridleway into the woods. Follow the path as it bears to the right away from the car park. Stay on this main path ignoring turnings to the left and right.

1. After fifteen minutes you will come to a fork in the road. Take the left-hand fork downhill and pass round the side of a wooden gate. In a few minutes you will see the reservoir ahead. Turn right onto the track so that you have the reservoir on your left and Swinsty Hall on your right.

   After ten minutes turn left and cross the reservoir dam (Swinsty Embankment). Once you have crossed the dam you will see a house (Swinsty Cottage) on your right. Go straight ahead over a small bridge and follow the road straight on.

Swinsty Reservoir

Five minutes later turn left off the road onto the path that runs alongside the reservoir. After a while the grassy path opens out with views over the reservoir to your left.

2. Follow the path up to the gate, turn left on to the road and cross over the bridge. Immediately after the bridge turn left through a wooden gate back onto the reservoir path.

   There are picnic tables here if you fancy stopping for lunch.

3. Follow this gravel path for twenty minutes until you see some steps up ahead. Ignore the steps and follow the path round to the right up to a gate. Turn left immediately before the gate along the path between the fence and the wall.

   Cross over the road, turn left onto the pavement and go over the dam between Swinsty and Fewston Reservoirs. At the end of the dam, cross back over the road onto the left-hand pavement and head up the hill back to the car park.

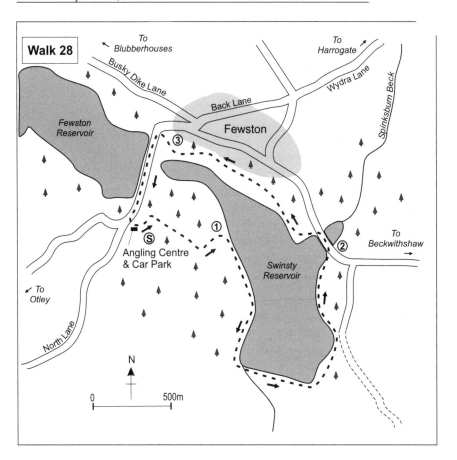

In the area:

Playdays Play & Party Centre, Otley (01943 468544). A soft play zone for toddlers, with a ball pit and lots of climbing apparatus. The café serves basic food and drinks. There are toilets with baby changing facilities. Open Tuesday to Saturday from 9.30am.

Harewood House (www.harewood.org; 0113 2181010). There is plenty to do at this stately home owned by the Queen's cousin the Earl of Harewood. Take a walk round the grounds, visit the bird garden, go on a boat trip or play in the adventure playground. Take a look inside Harewood House itself and see the huge art collection, the staterooms and the below-stairs exhibition. Open from March between 10.00am-6.00pm but check the website for more accurate details.

⚔ 29: Ripley Castle and Hollybank Wood

Allow: *1 hour 15 minutes*

Ripley Castle sits in the picturesque village of Ripley and has been home to the Ingilby family for the last 700 years. The Ingilbys have been closely associated with the Monarchy over that time; however, it has been a turbulent relationship. James I stayed at the castle in 1603 but within two years the Ingilbys were plotting to kill him. Nine of the eleven conspirators associated with the Gunpowder Plot were close relations or associates of the family.

This simple walk takes you down Hollybank Lane, past the castle and into the beautiful Hollybank Wood. Hollybank Lane formed part of the Roman road between Ilkley and the garrison town at Aldborough, near Boroughbridge. Some of the original paving is still visible in places. Hollybank Wood is lovely all year round but especially beautiful in May when it is filled with bluebells and during the autumn leaf fall. Great views can be seen over Nidderdale from many points along this route.

Map: Ordnance Survey 1:25000 Explorer 298 – grid reference 284603

Distance: 2½ miles

Getting there: Park in the free car park in Ripley. There are grassy areas with picnic tables here and toilets with baby changing facilities.

Go through the kissing gate at the end of the car park and turn left onto the pavement. Turn left just before the Boar's Head signposted to Ripley Castle and Gardens and the Castle Tea Rooms. There is an old stone cross and stocks just in front of the pub. You will then walk past All Saints Church on your left.

1. Walk past the Castle entrance on your right and simply continue

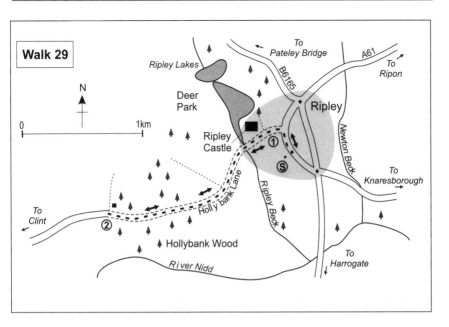

walking straight ahead over some cobblestones and onto Hollybank Lane. The castle wall will be on your immediate right. This broad gravel lane takes you down over Ripley Beck. As you go over the bridge you will see a water cascade and iron bridge on your right.

Take a look over the castle wall after the bridge for great views of the Castle itself.

Continue along the track until you reach a fork. Take the left-hand path towards Hollybank Lodge and Clint. Soon you will enter Hollybank Wood.

There is a bench if you want to stop and absorb the tranquil atmosphere. Keep an eye out for wildlife as you may see deer as you walk along.

2. Finally you will reach a gate with Hollybank Lodge on the right. This is the turning point for the walk. It is possible to walk all the way to Clint but there isn't much to do when you get there! So simply turn round and retrace your steps.

Ripley Castle

In the area:

Ripley Castle (www.ripleycastle.co.uk; 01423 770152). Take a stroll round the extensive castle gardens, go on the park walk and see the fallow deer and cattle grazing, or take the kids to the children's play area. Tours around the castle itself leave every 30 minutes and take around 1 hour 15 minutes. There are special castle tours for children between the ages of 5-13 during the summer holidays. Refreshments can be found in the castle tea rooms. The castle is open daily between June and September but check the website for opening times during the rest of the year. The gardens are open daily throughout the year.

Mother Shipton's Cave (www.mothershiptonscave.com; 01423 864600). Mother Shipton is England's most famous prophetess who lived 500 years ago. The cave is her legendary birthplace and is open daily between March and October. Close by is the Petrifying Well which is believed to be the only well of its kind in England. The well was believed to have great healing powers. Also on site are woodland and riverside walks, tea rooms, an adventure playground and trail quiz.

Walk 30: Nidd Gorge, Harrogate

Allow: *1 hour or 2 hours 30 minutes*

Nidd Gorge is a wildlife haven which once formed part of a royal hunting park from the days of King John in the 13th century. This is a beautiful and tranquil stretch of the river and a great place to relax. The first part of the walk follows the route of the old Harrogate gasworks railway 'Barber Line' which was in use from 1907-1956 carrying coal and bitumen. This walk follows dirt tracks along the wooded river bank. The paths can become very muddy and may flood when there has been lots of rain.

I have suggested two possible routes. The first is an easy walk along decent tracks. The second is a much longer walk through Nidd Gorge nature reserve which is not for the faint hearted. This is a beautiful but difficult route which involves lifting the pushchair over three stiles.

Map: Ordnance Survey 1:25000 Explorer 297 – grid reference 313576

Distance: 2 or 4½ miles

Getting there: Park in the car park on Bilton Lane.

Cross the road and immediately in front of you is an information board with details about the area. Go through the wooden barrier to the left of the sign and follow the bridleway along this dismantled railway path. On the left of this track you can see Bilton and to the right are grass fields. Stay on this main track until you reach a T-junction with the river gorge ahead of you.

> The viaduct ahead is part of the old railway which allowed the trains to cross over Nidd gorge

1. Turn right walking with Nidd gorge on your left and a grassy field on your right. Follow the left-hand edge of this field until you come to the far left-hand corner where there is an opening into

the woodland. There is a sign here marked as Bilton Beck and Rudding Bottoms.

After a few minutes you will see the River Nidd on your left. Keep following the path straight ahead as it goes down a short steep slope. Cross the footbridge over Bilton Beck and keep following the path ahead. The path follows the river bank and boarding has been laid over much of the route in order to make the path more accessible.

You will soon come to a fork in the path. The left-hand fork just

Boardwalk through Nidd Gorge

takes you to a view point over the weir. So take the right-hand path which takes you up a short uphill and along through the woodland. As this is a woodland path you will have to negotiate your way around the odd tree root and rock but on the whole the path is easy to push along.

The path takes you to a wooden fence with a narrow gap to walk through. If you look to the left you can see that it is easy to take the pushchair round the edge of the fence and back up onto the path.

2. Soon you will reach a junction, Milners fork.

**** To do the short walk turn right here up the hill and follow this bridleway all the way back to Bilton Lane. When you reach

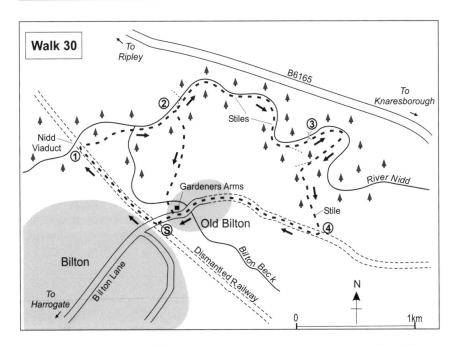

Bilton Lane you will see the Gardeners pub on your left. Turn right here and follow the road along until you see the car park on your left.

The long walk requires two people as there are three stiles. Turn left along the path which is signed to Knaresborough. Almost immediately you will come to another fork where you take the path to the right. The path brings you back down to the river where you turn right through the wooden gate and walk along with the river on your left. The path then splits and weaves its way along the river bank for a while, so find the best route for you making sure you don't stray far from the river.

Cross over the first stile and follow the path ahead. This takes you across a short section of uneven stone slab path which then returns to a boarded path. You will soon come to a clearing in the woodland where you must continue to follow the river bank.

There are several small beach areas along the river which make lovely picnic spots but make sure you bring something to sit on.

Soon you will come to another stile, cross this and continue straight ahead. You are then heading back into the woodland of Bilton banks. Ignore paths off to the right and continue straight ahead. Go up a short rocky uphill section of the path and then over a narrow wooden plank bridge. Keep following the main path along the river side.

3. You will soon see a footbridge over the river on your left, do not cross this but continue following the path along the river bank. When you come to a bench you will see a series of wooden steps. With a bit of negotiation you can take the pushchair to the side of the steps. The path continues uphill into woodland away from the river and up a second stepped area. Once you are up the worst of this uphill there is a small bench where you can stop for a breather.

Continue straight ahead at the next junction marked with yellow footpath arrows and not on the path to the right. This takes you up to the top edge of the woodland where you will see a metal gate on your right. Keep following the footpath to the left through the wood.

After 5-10 minutes you will come to a wooden gate and the final stile. Lift the pushchair over this and follow the track up to the road.

4. Go through the metal gate, turn right and walk along this gravel lane (Bilton Lane). The lane soon changes from gravel to tarmac and simply follow this lane all the way back to your car. On your way you will pass Bilton Park Village Farm Caravan Park on your right and the Gardeners Arms which has a large beer garden. Immediately after the pub you will see a bridleway on the right which is the route that the short walk takes. A few minutes after this you will see the car park on your left.

In the area:

Newby Hall (www.newbyhall.co.uk; 0845 4504068). This is the family home of the Comptons and is one of England's renowned

Adam houses. The house was built in the 17th century under the guidance of Sir Christopher Wren and now has fine examples of tapestries, statues and some of Chippendale's finest furniture. The house is set in 25 acres of gardens and is a fantastic place for the whole family to explore. There is an adventure garden for the kids, miniature railway, sculpture park and woodland walk. Refreshments can be found in the restaurant or take a picnic. The house and gardens are open daily between April and September between 11.00am-5.30pm.

The Time Machine, Harrogate (www.childrenstimemachine.co.uk; 01423 816111). This is an indoor adventure soft play and party centre. The apparatus includes lots of exciting climbing structures and educational toys. There is a dinosaur-themed area, a multi-level gym shaped as a medieval castle, a space station and ride on cars. There is a café, a microwave for warming meals and bottles and toilets with baby-changing facilities. Suitable for children between the ages of 4 months to 10 years. Open seven days a week 10.00am-6.00pm.

More books for intrepid pushchair walkers!

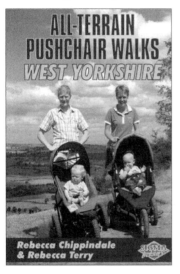

ALL-TERRAIN PUSHCHAIR WALKS: WEST YORKSHIRE

Rebecca Chippindale & Rebecca Terry

Pushchair-friendly routes in the spectacular countryside around the major towns of Keighley, Bradford, Leeds, Halifax, Huddersfield and Wakefield. Walks visit a wide variety of locations including Ilkley Moor, Hardcastle Crags, Hebden Bridge and the River Wharfe. *£7.95*

ALL-TERRAIN PUSHCHAIR WALKS: SNOWDONIA

Zoë Sayer & Rebecca Terry

30 pushchair-friendly walks through the spectacular scenery of the Snowdonia National Park. The walks range from simple riverside strolls to full-on alpine-style stomps. *£7.95*

ALL-TERRAIN PUSHCHAIR WALKS: ANGLESEY & LLEYN PENINSULA

Zoë Sayer & Rebecca Terry

Also by Zoë and Rebecca, 30 pushchair-friendly walks in this popular tourist area. Countryside and coastal routes galore! *£7.95*

ALL-TERRAIN PUSHCHAIR WALKS: PEAK DISTRICT

Alison Southern

Level routes around Peak District villages and more adventurous (but safe) hikes across the moors. Alison is a parent of a young child and has an excellent knowledge of the Peak District. So now there's no reason to stay at home – here is the ideal opportunity to introduce the youngest children to the wide-open spaces of the Peak District! *£7.95*

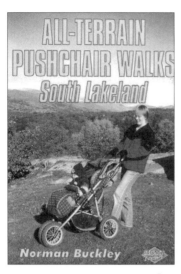

ALL-TERRAIN PUSHCHAIR WALKS: NORTH LAKELAND

Ruth & Richard Irons

30 walks across North Lakeland from Ennerdale Water to Lowther Park, Haweswater to Bassenthwaite. Something to suit every type of walker – from Sunday Strollers to Peak Baggers and everyone else in between! Ruth and Richard Irons are experienced parents and qualified outdoor pursuits instructors – a reliable combination! *£6.95*

ALL-TERRAIN PUSHCHAIR WALKS: SOUTH LAKELAND

Norman Buckley

"This book is fantastic - a perfect guide for parents" — *Kathleen Jones (Lakeland Book of The Year Awards, 2005).* The companion to our 'All-Terrain Pushchair Walks for North Lakeland' – walks north to south, from Grasmere to Grizedale Forest, and west to east, from Coniston to Kendal - you'll be spoilt for choice! *£6.95*

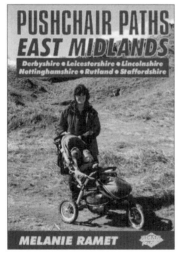

PUSHCHAIR PATHS: EAST MIDLANDS

Melanie Ramet

This is the first pushchair-friendly walking book for the East Midlands written by enthusiastic walker, writer and 'East Midlander', Melanie Ramet.

Melanie has written 25 'ORPing' (Off-Road Pushchairing) routes to encourage unrestricted access into the heart of the wonderful East Midlands countryside, where walkers can be confident there will be no unexpected obstacles to negotiate the pushchair over, under or through! *£7.95*

All of our books are all available through booksellers. For a free catalogue, please contact: **SIGMA LEISURE, 5 ALTON ROAD, WILMSLOW, CHESHIRE SK9 5DY**

Tel/Fax: 01625-531035

E-mail: info@sigmapress.co.uk   Web site: www.sigmapress.co.uk